Love one another

JUS-TICE

TO APPRECIATE PROPERLY

BY TISHA

JUS-TICE TO APPRECIATE PROPERLY

COPYRIGHT © 2013 BY TISHA

PUBLISHING, PHOTOS, DESIGNS AND EDITING BY: TISHA

TISHA, 1968-JUS-TICE TO APPRECIATE PROPERLY
LIBRARY OF CONGRESS CATALOGING IN PUBLICATION DATA: VAU-1-155-530
ISBN: 978-0-615-99199-3
10 9 8 7 6 5 4 3 2 1
1. PHOTOGRAPHY 2. VISUAL ART
(FIRST EDITION)

TISHA
4403 N. SACRAMENTO AVENUE
CHICAGO, IL 60625

SOFTCOVER EDITION 2014 PRINTED IN THE U.S.A BY CREATESPACE

EPIGRAPH:

IT IS NOT NECESSARY
TO KNOW THE
NOMENCLATURES OF THE
FOLLOWING ITEMS, THEIR PURPOSE IS TO
PROMPT US ALL TO LOOK.
THEY ARE MEANT;
TO PROMPT US ALL TO REALLY SEE,
TO GIVE JUSTICE,
AND TO
APPRECIATE PROPERLY,
ALL THE WONDERFUL THINGS AROUND US.

INTRODUCTION:

FROM ANOTHER WORLD YOU ARE....

TO ME, FROM ME AND FOR ALL THE WORLD

TO SEE....

THE FOLLOWING PICTURES ARE A SAMPLE OF THE MANY

FASCINATING THINGS THAT A HUMBLE SOUL HAS NOTICED.

THINGS THAT DESERVE CLOSER OBSERVATION AND

AWARENESS OF THE WORLD AND OBJECTS AROUND US. THESE

BEAUTIFUL SIGHTS

AND MANY MORE ARE SOMETIMES TAKEN FOR GRANTED. IT IS MY

HOPE....

THAT WE WILL ALL PAY MORE ATTENTION TO NATURES' BEAUTY, UP

CLOSE, AND WITH AN UNDERSTANDING OF THE MANY THINGS WE DO

NOT KNOW AND CANNOT SEE. I HOPE YOU LIKE THEM.

FINALLY, IT IS MY HOPE THAT YOU WILL GIVE THEM....

JUS-TICE AND APPRECIATE THEM PROPERLY.

IN THE MVSKOKE CREEK LANGUAGE; HECKETV (TO BE BORN)

AND HECETV (TO SEE), CONVERGE TO (BORN TO SEE). THESE WORDS ARE

POWERFUL TO ME AND IN GRATITUDE THIS BOOK PAYS

HOMAGE TO ALL WHO TRY.

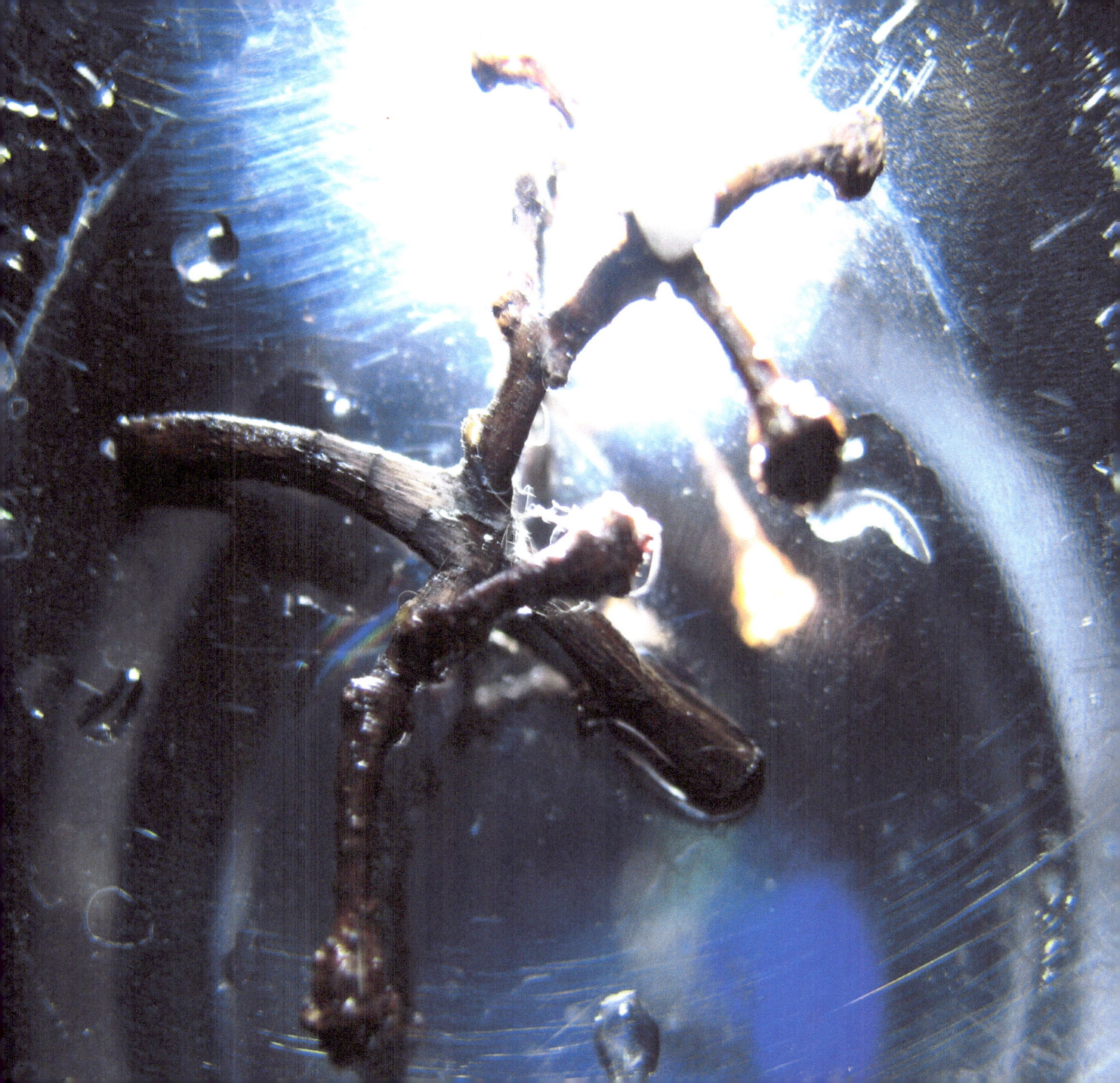

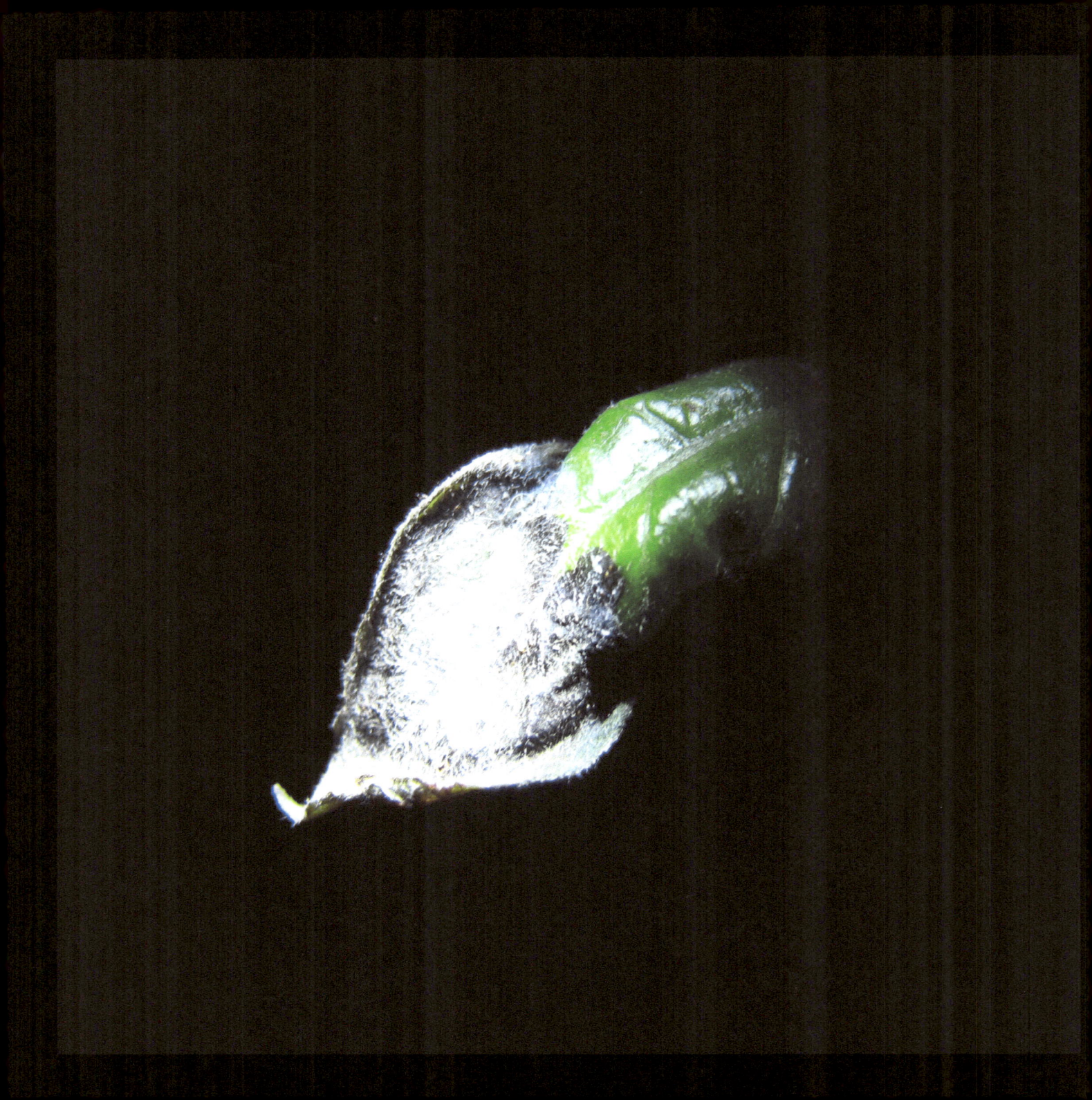

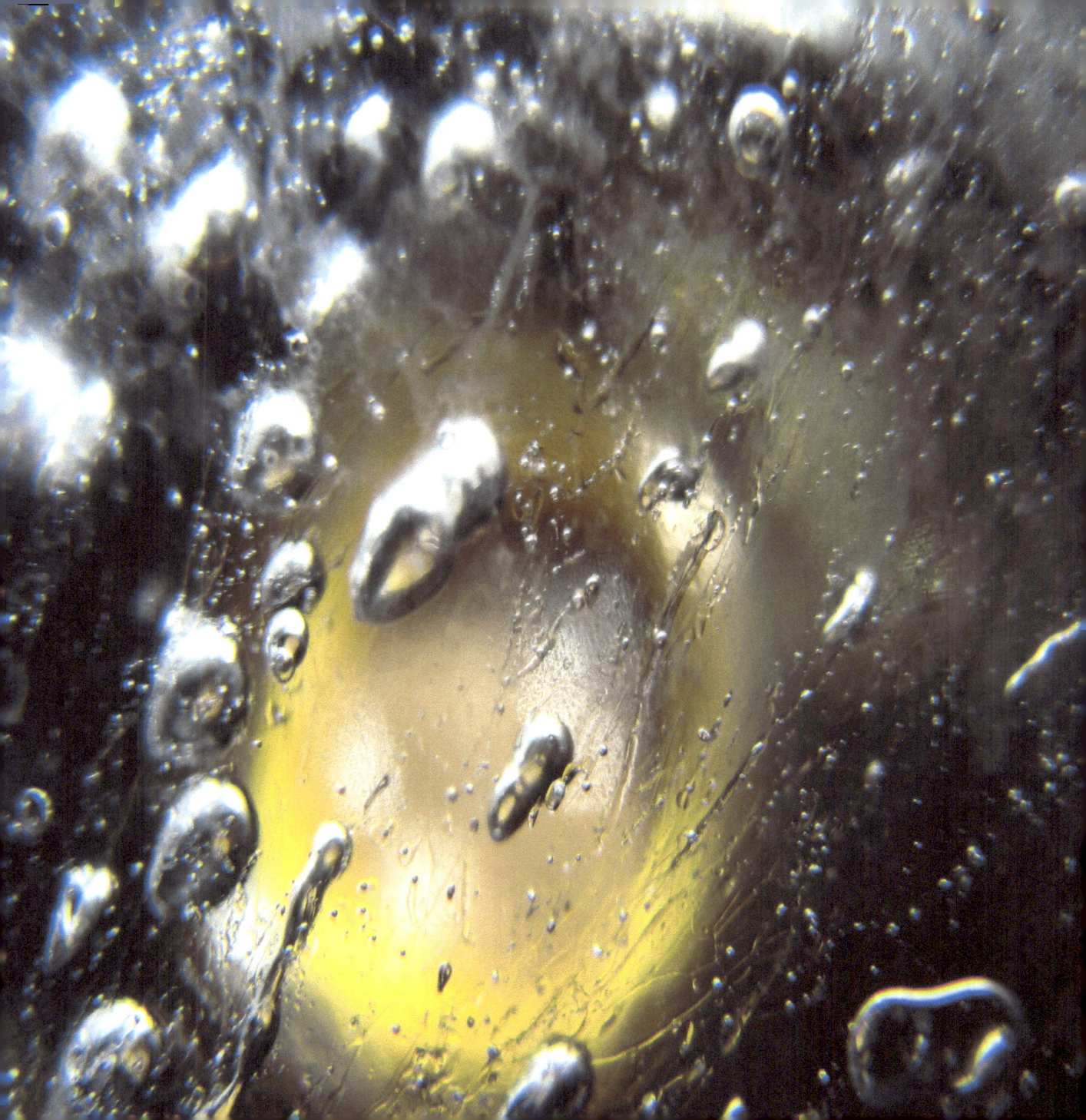

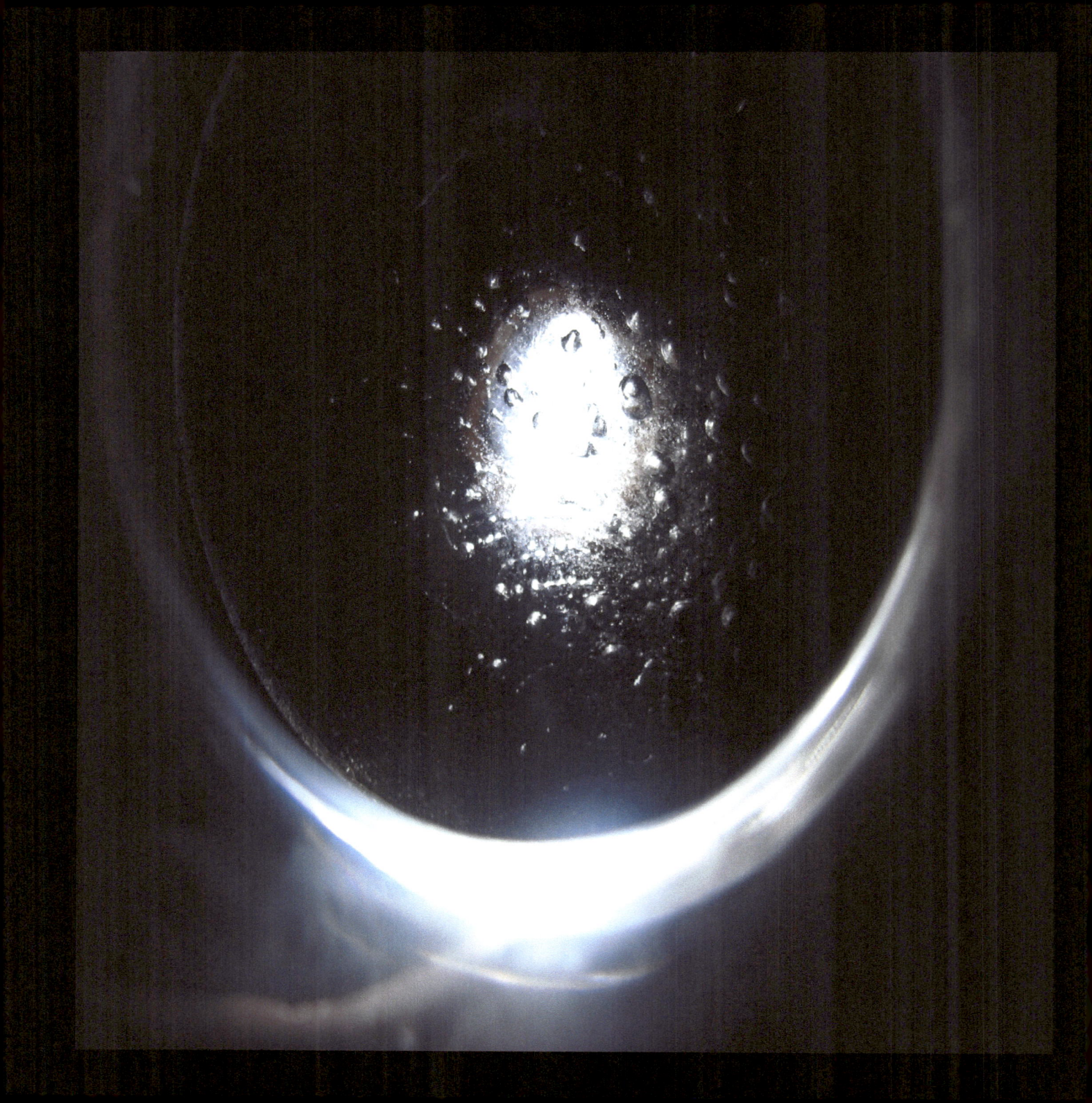

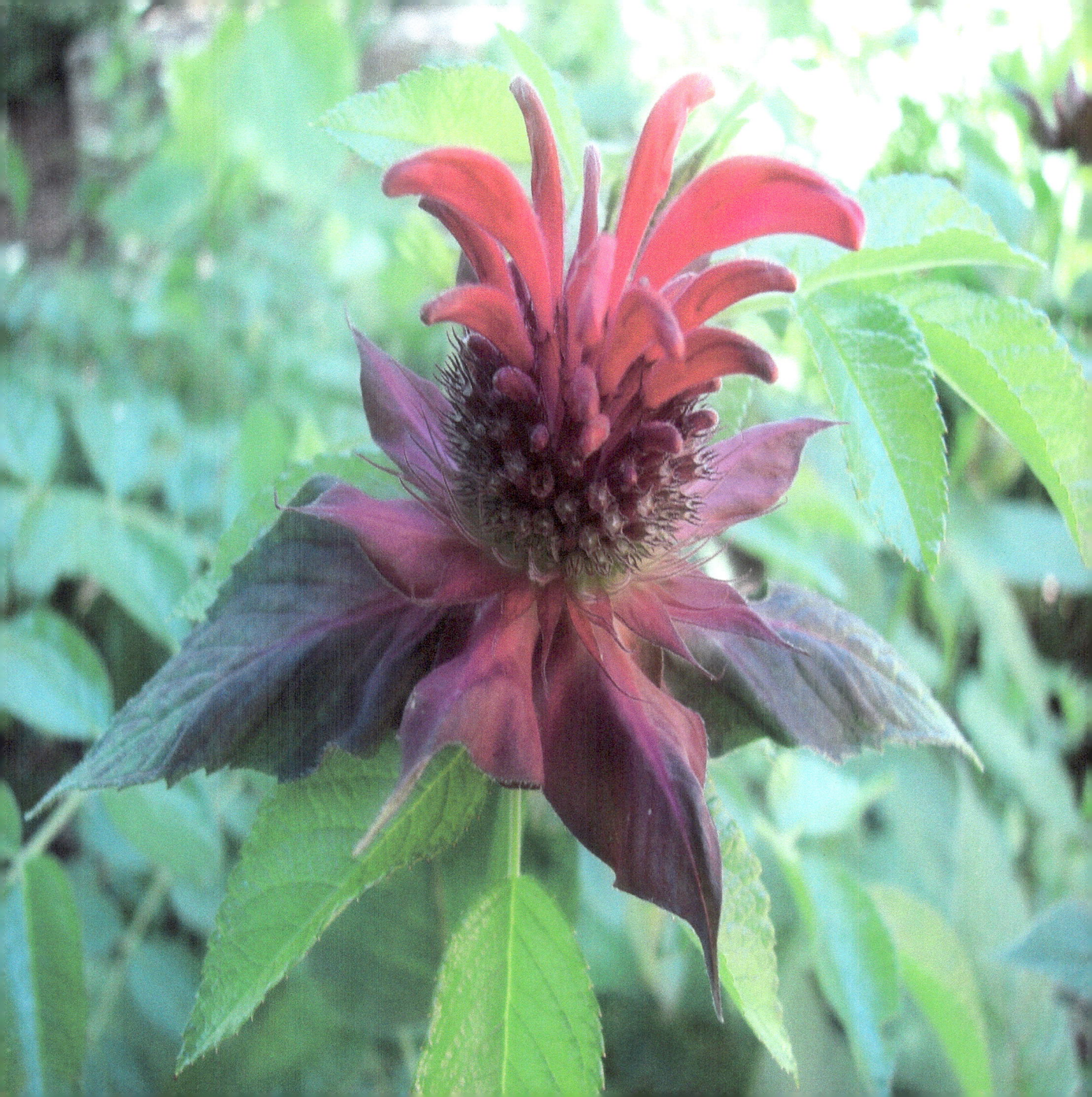

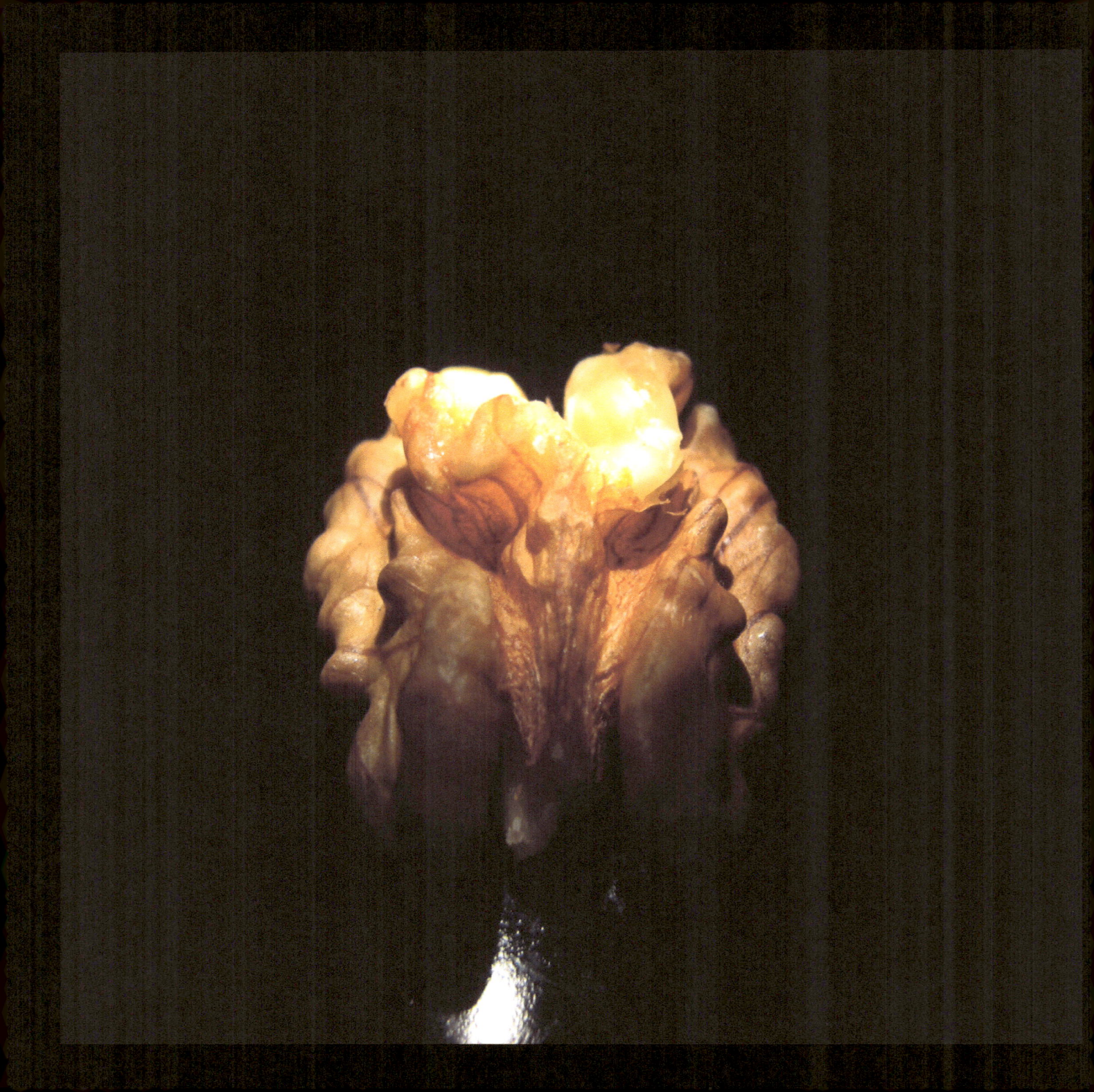

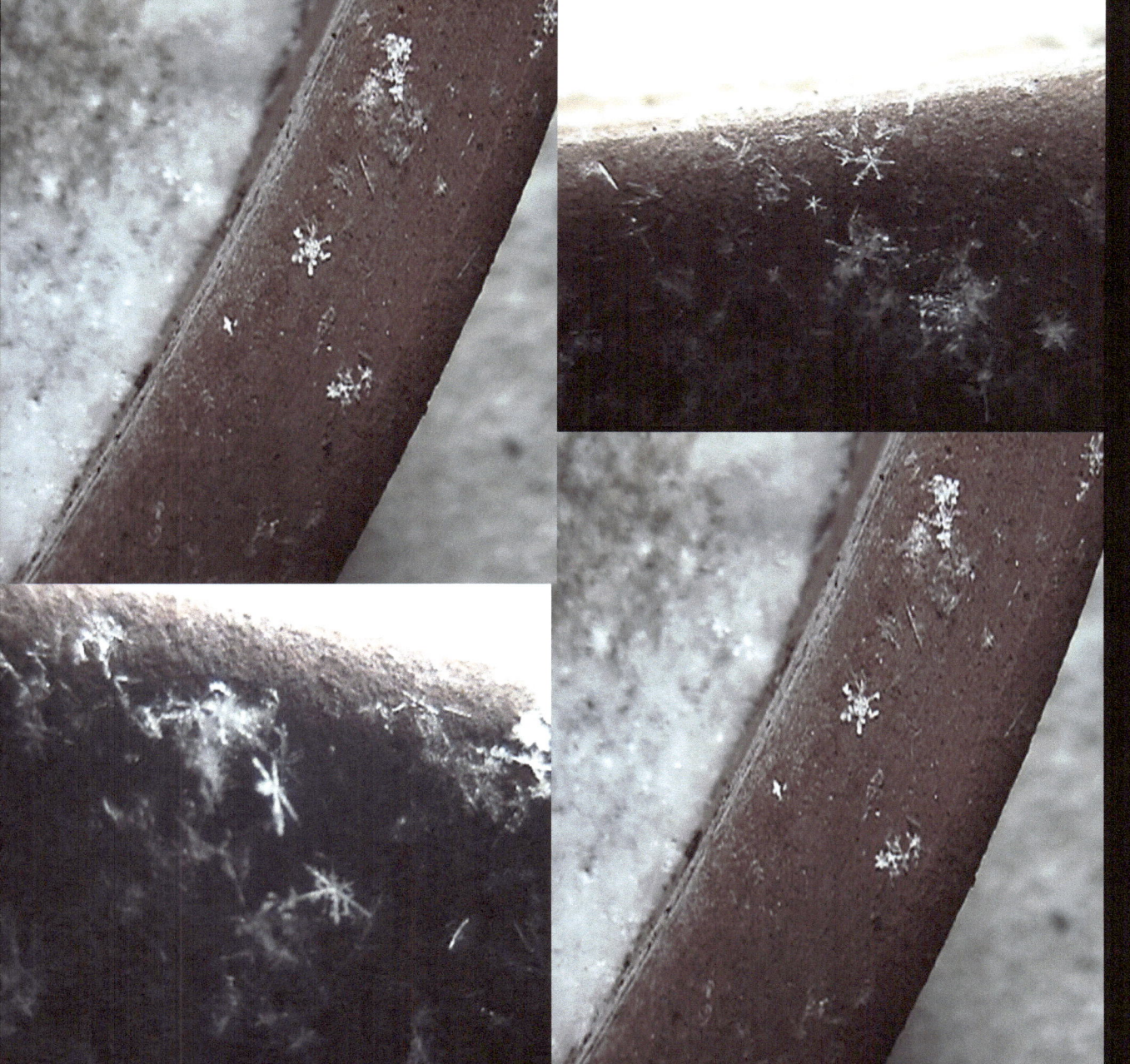

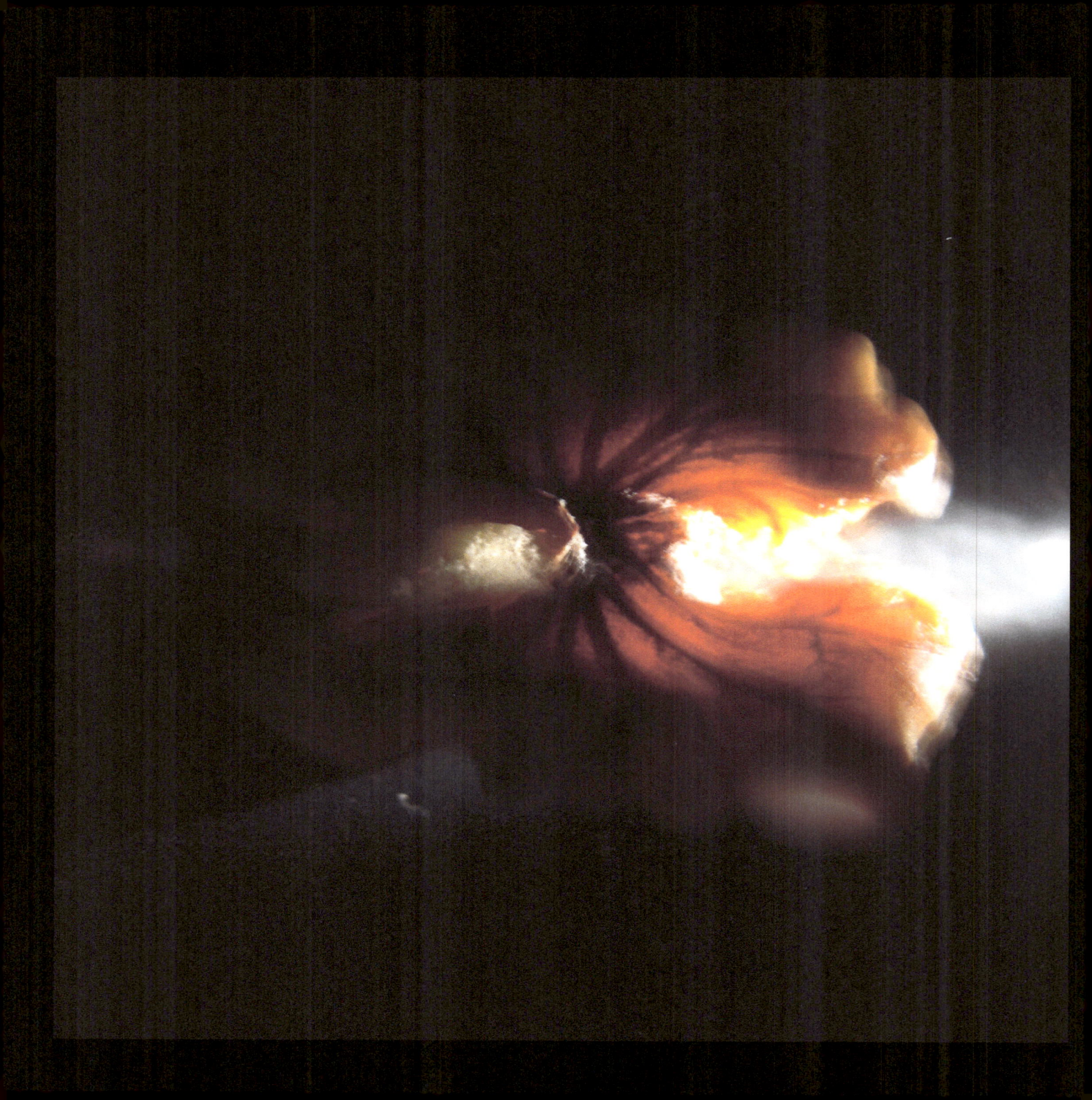

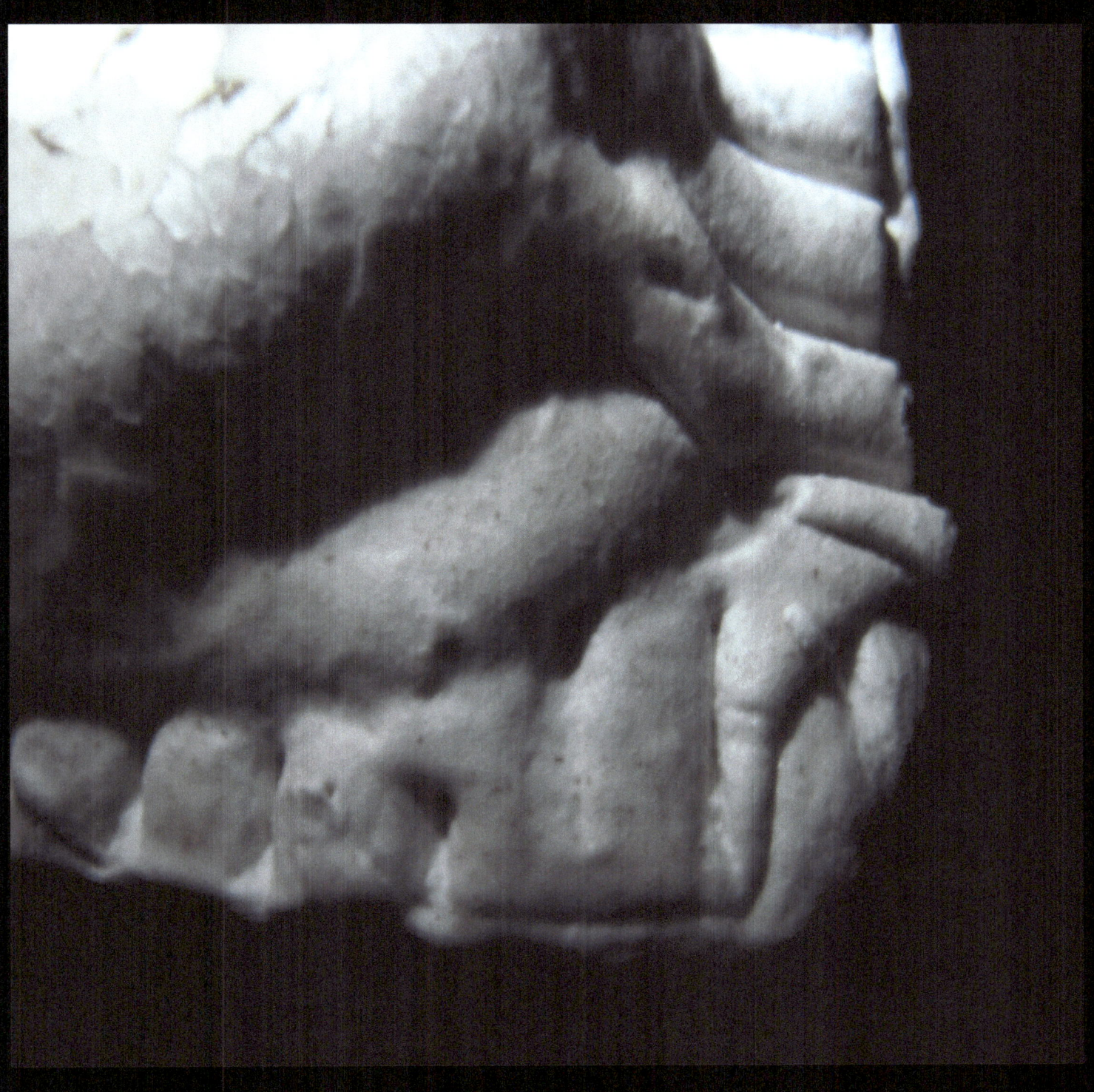

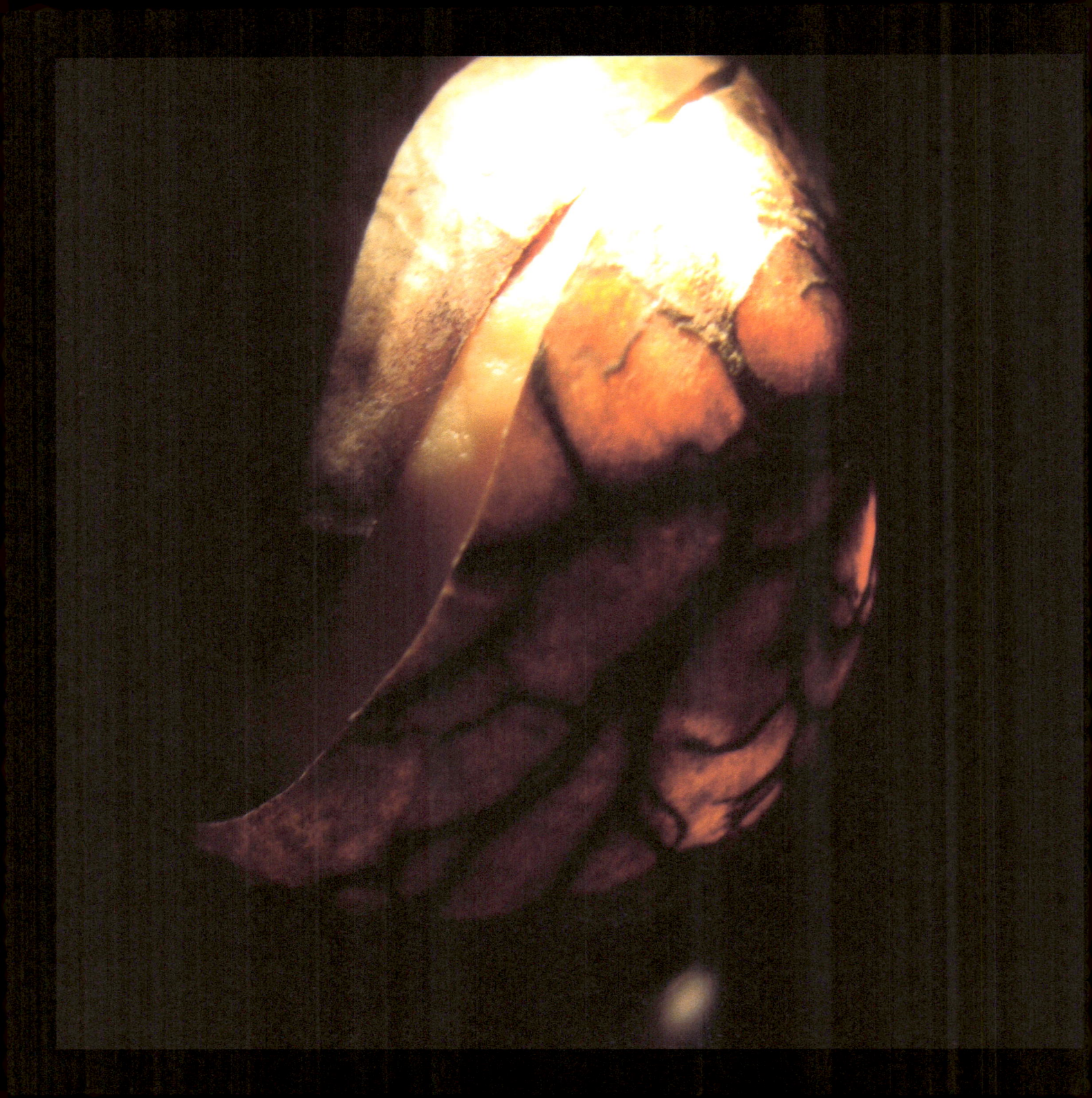

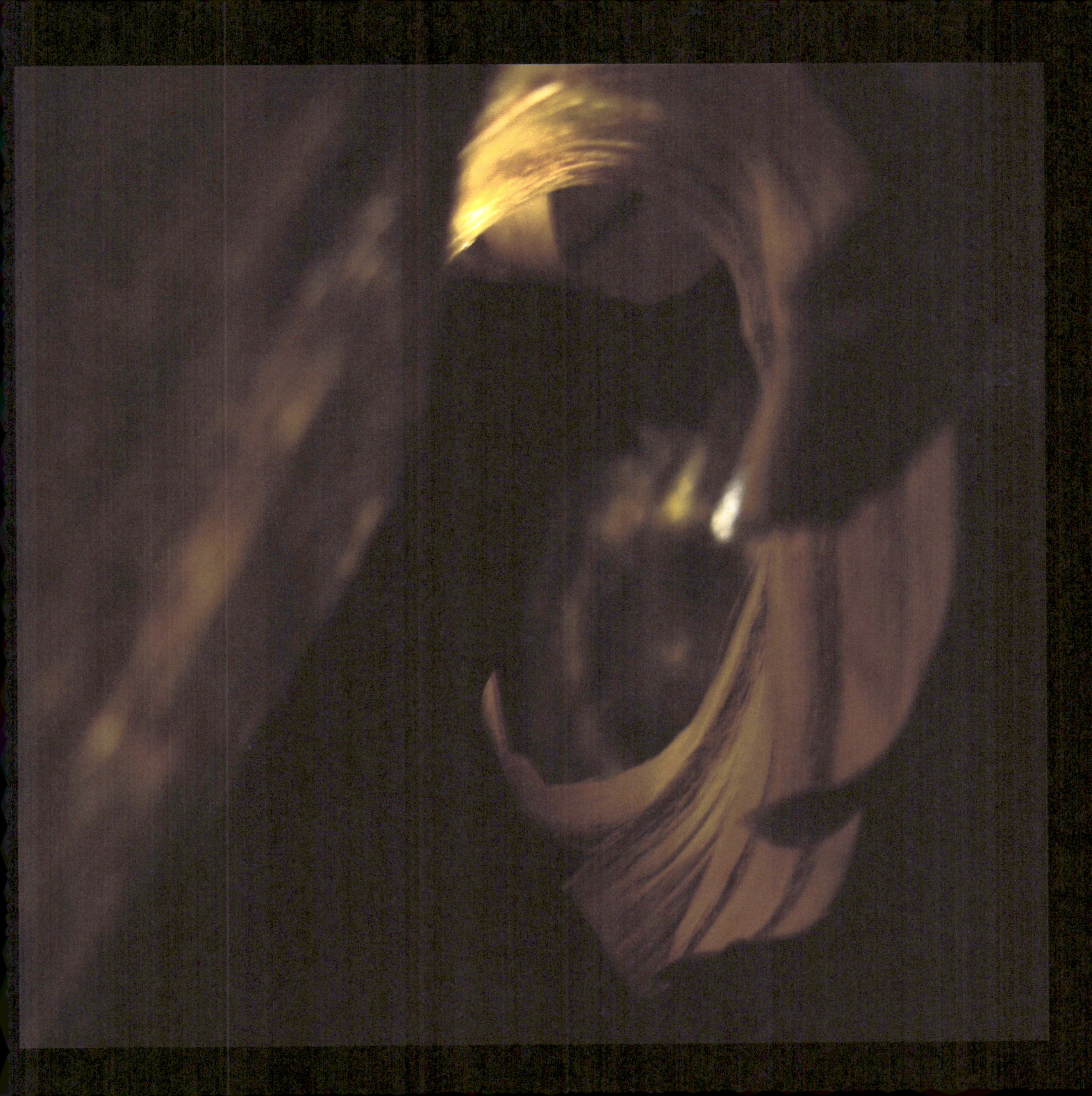

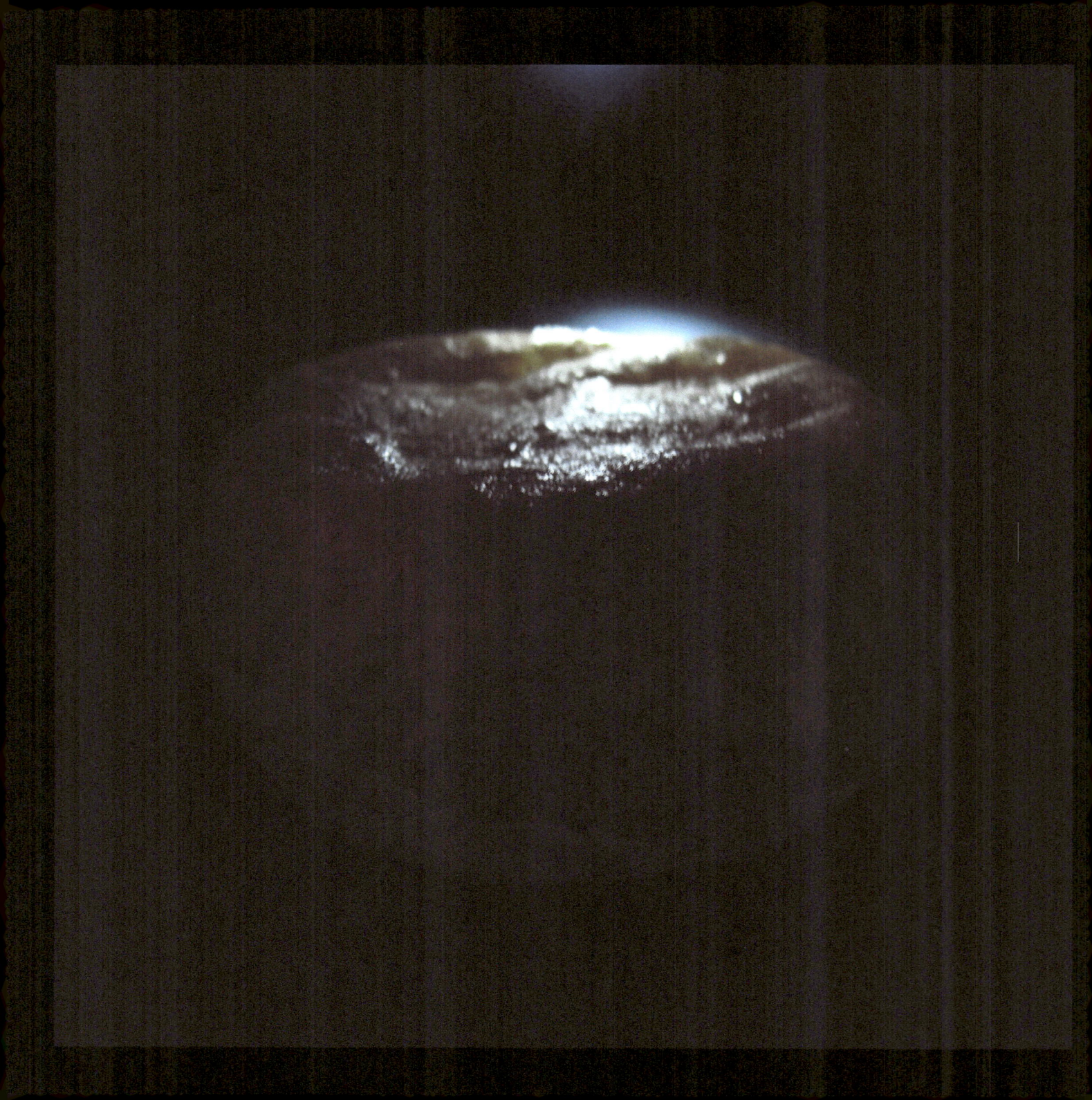

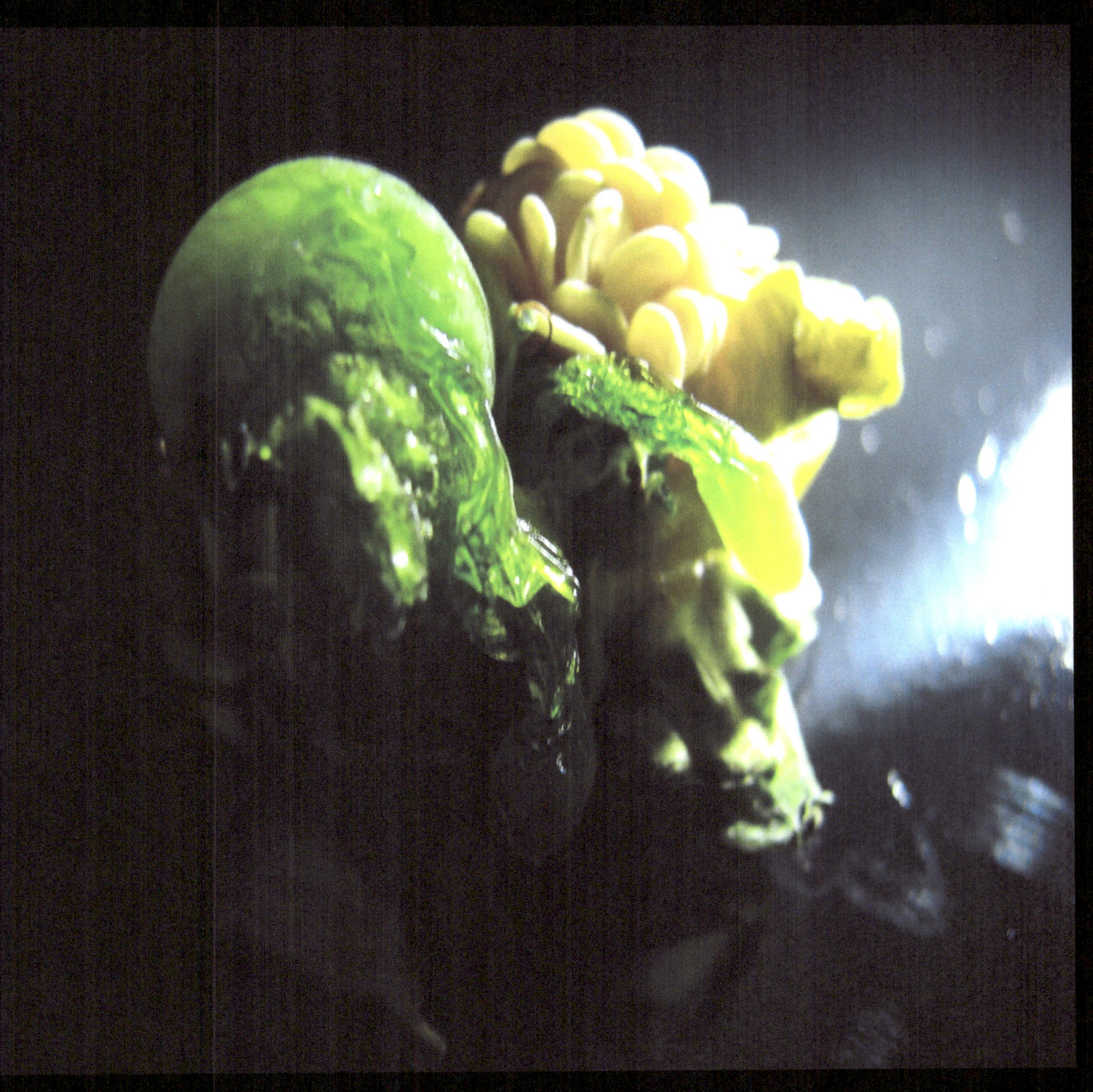

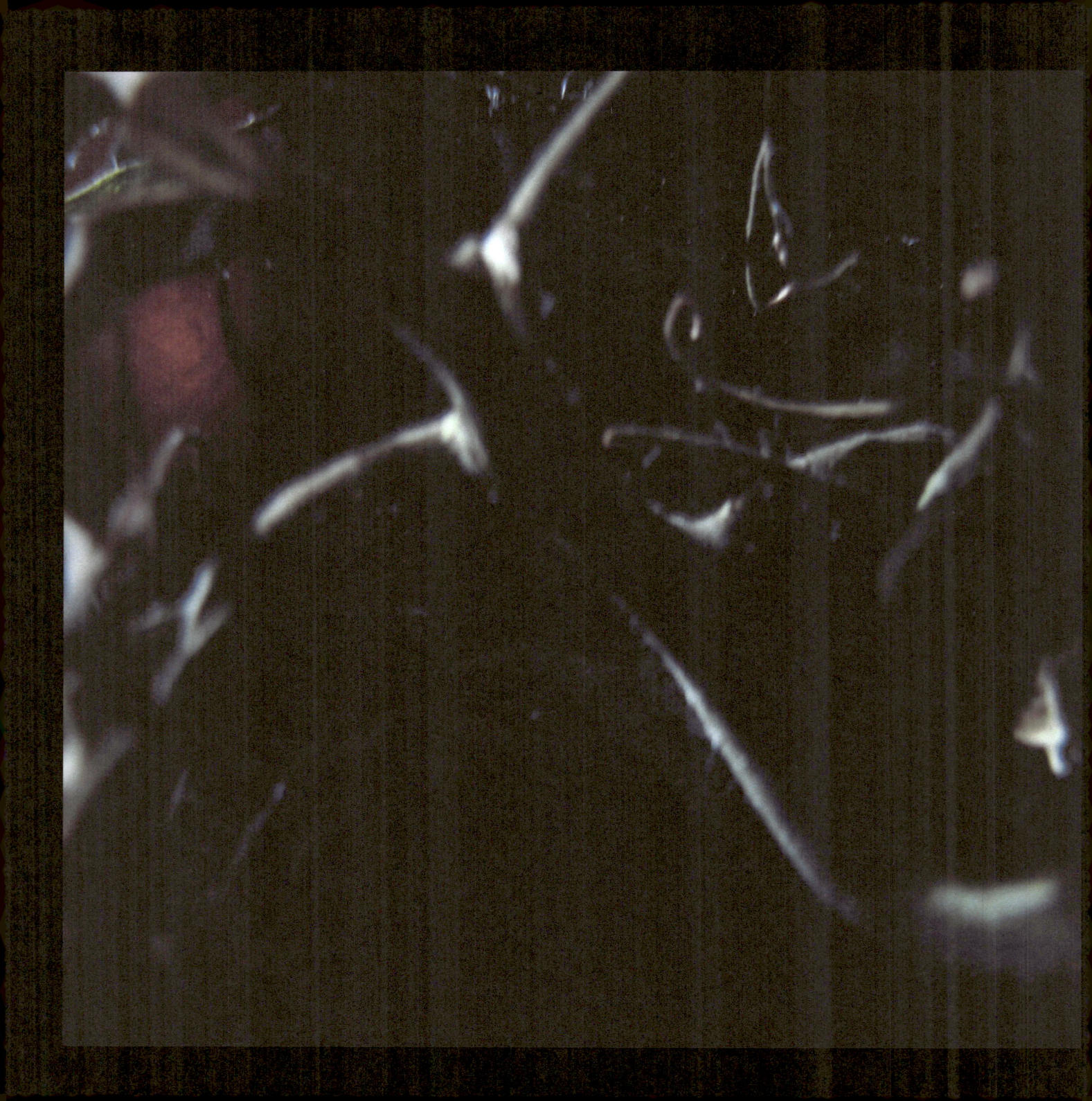

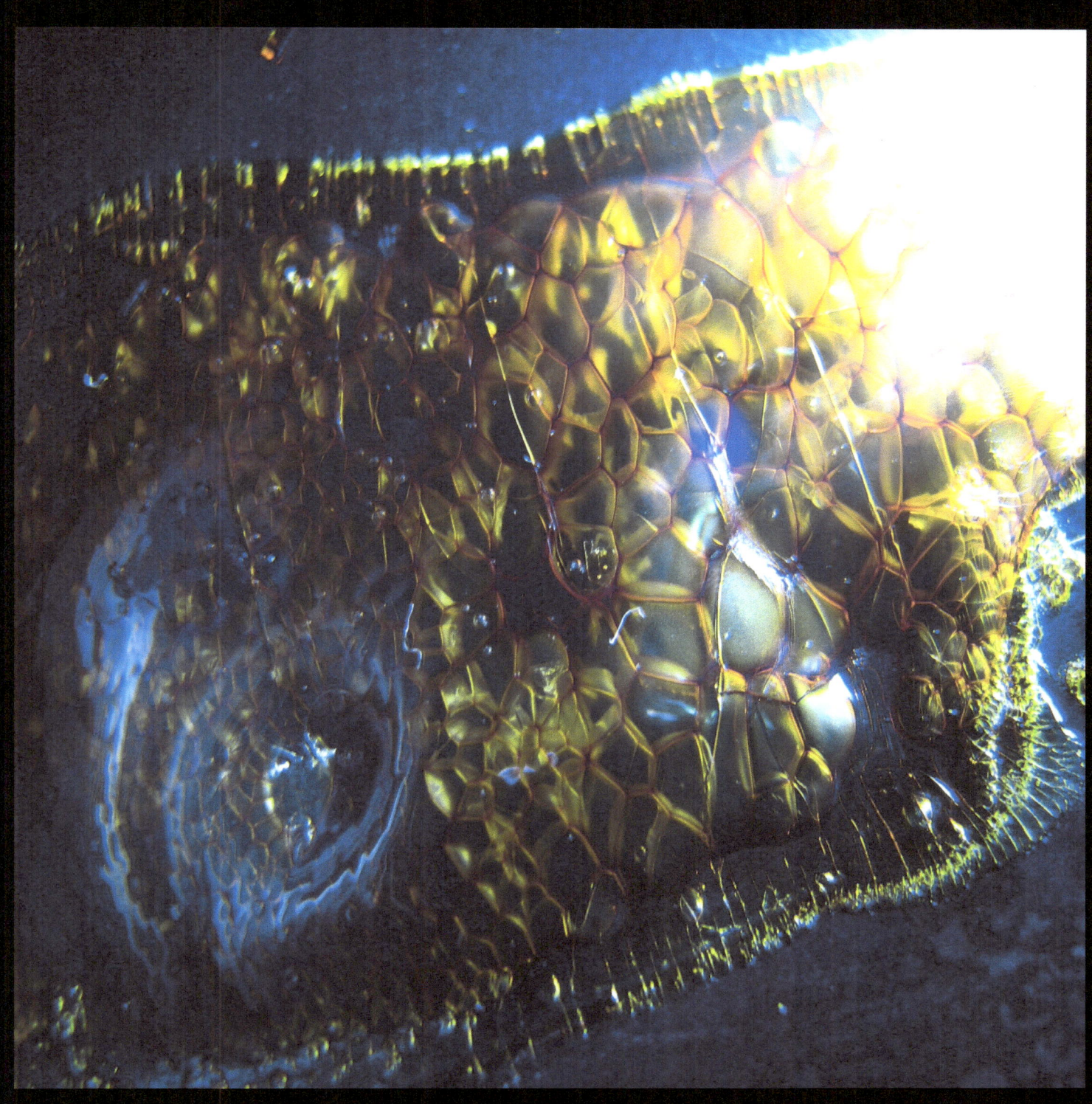

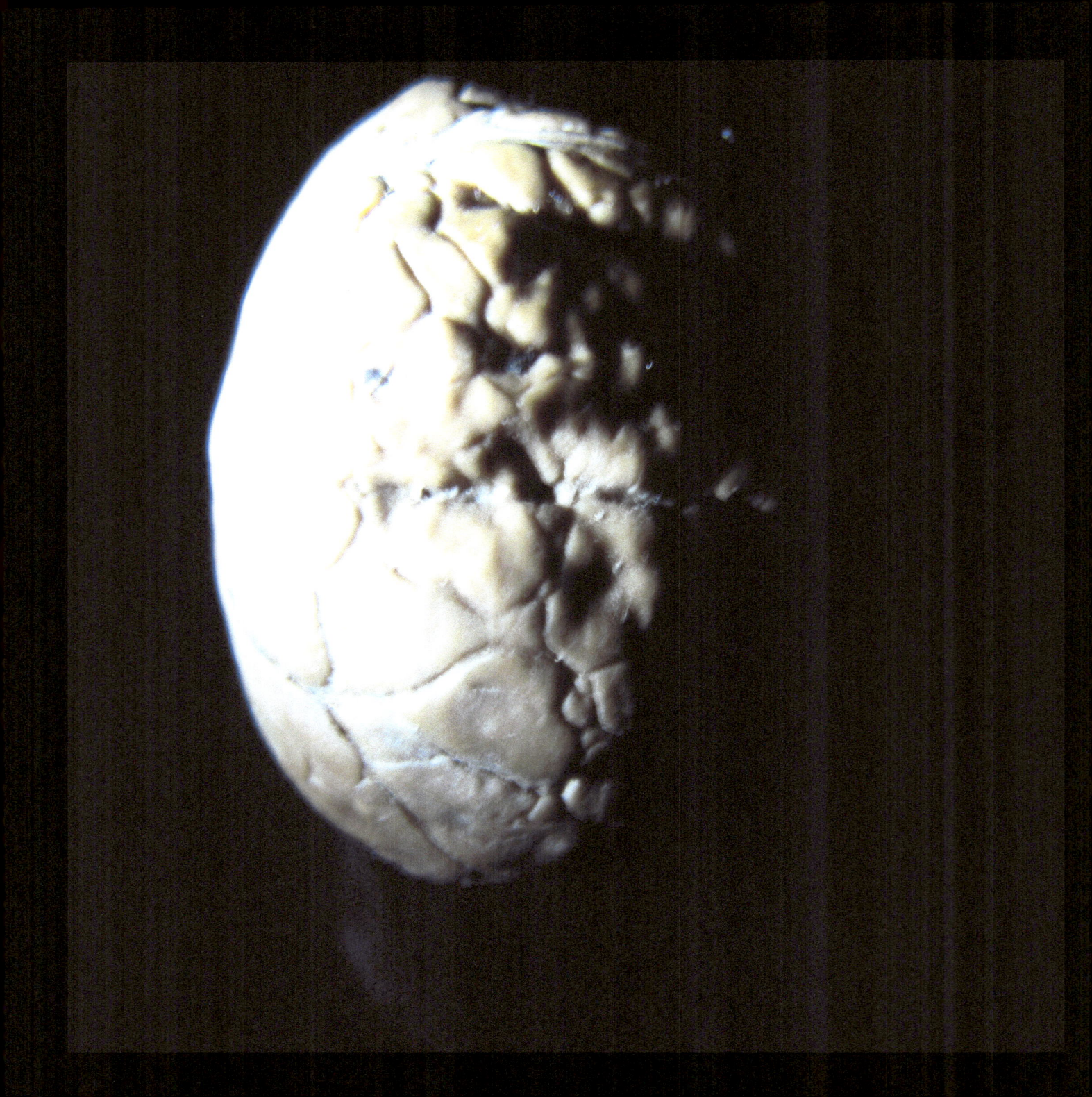

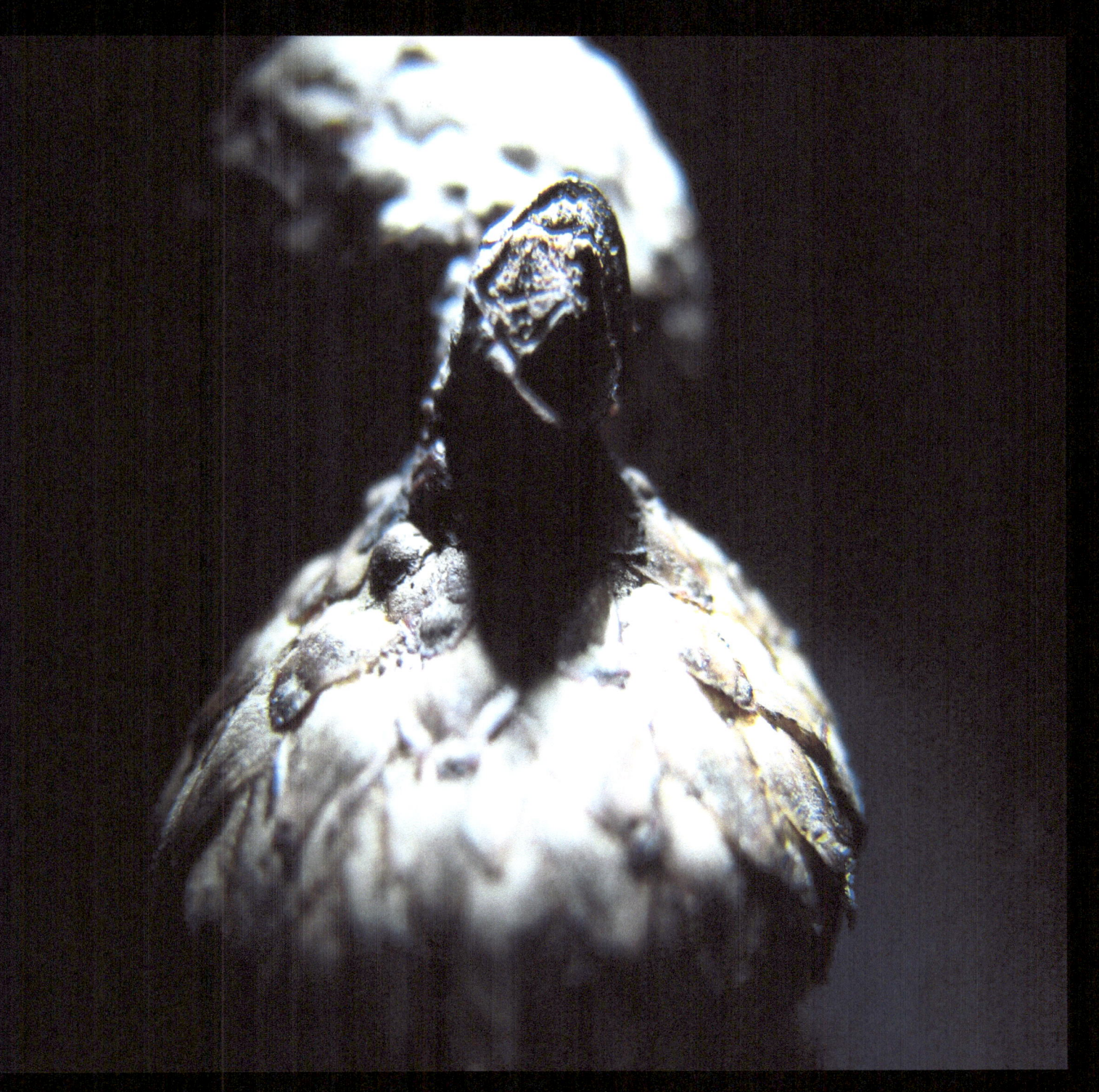

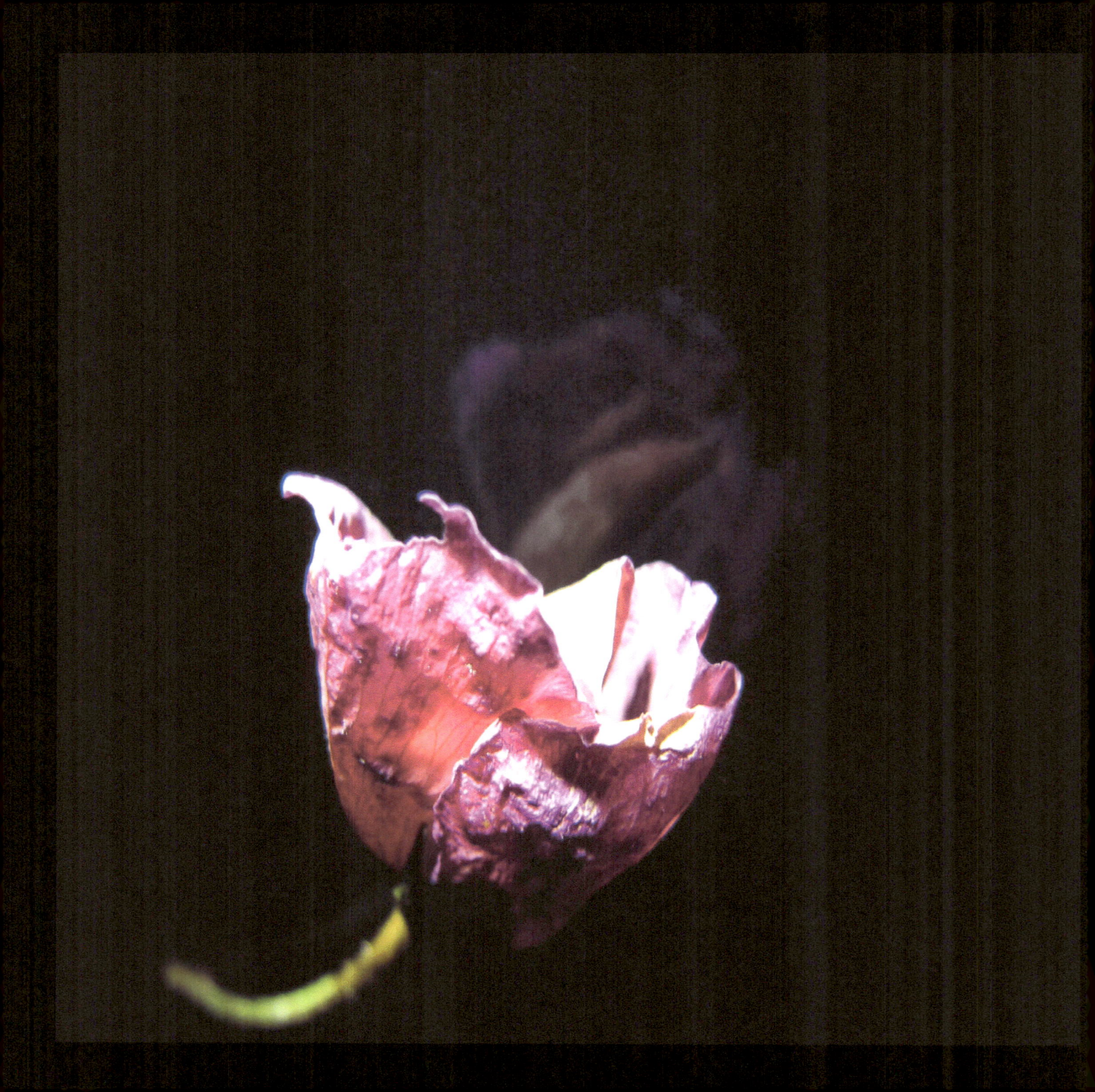

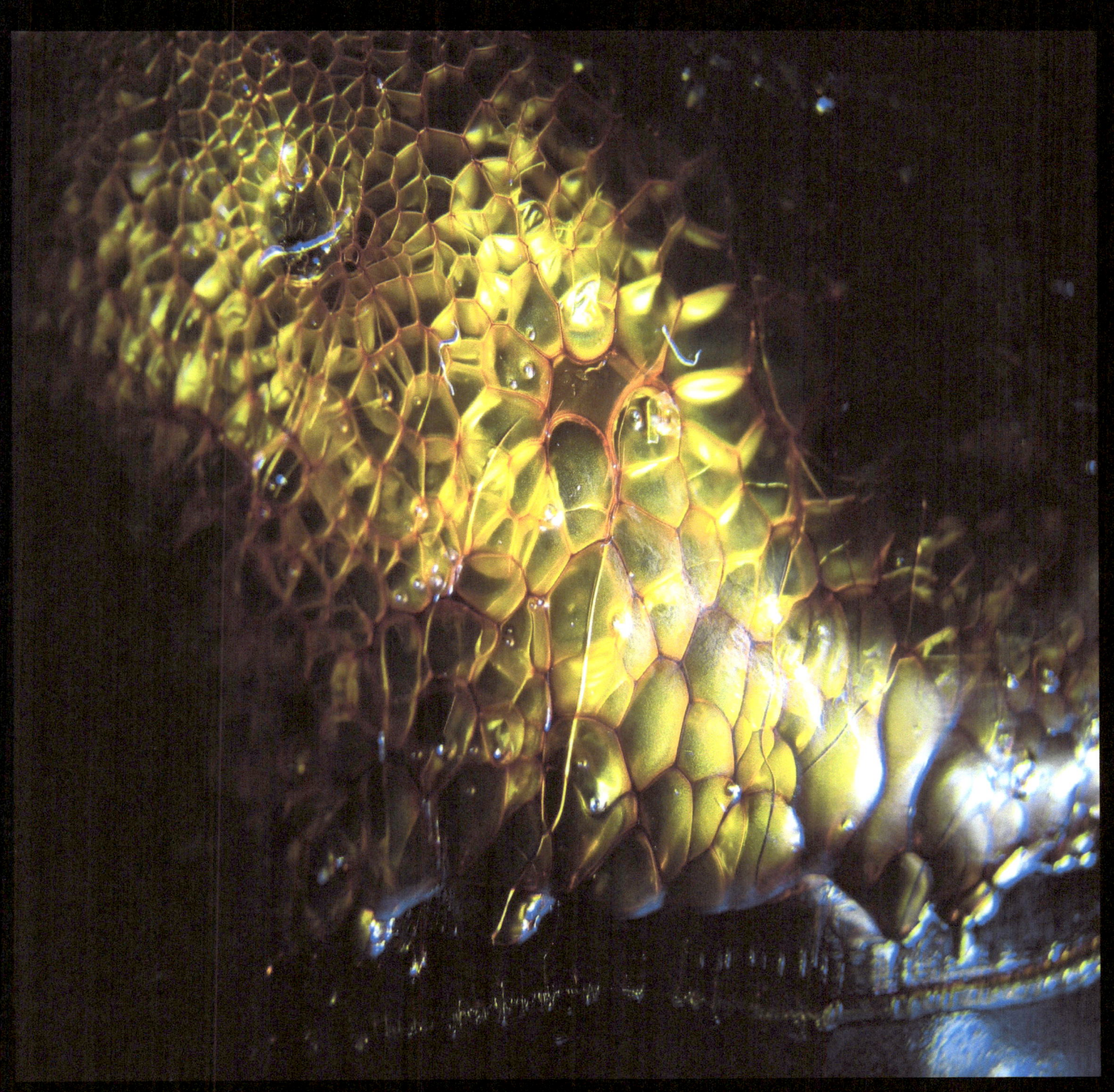

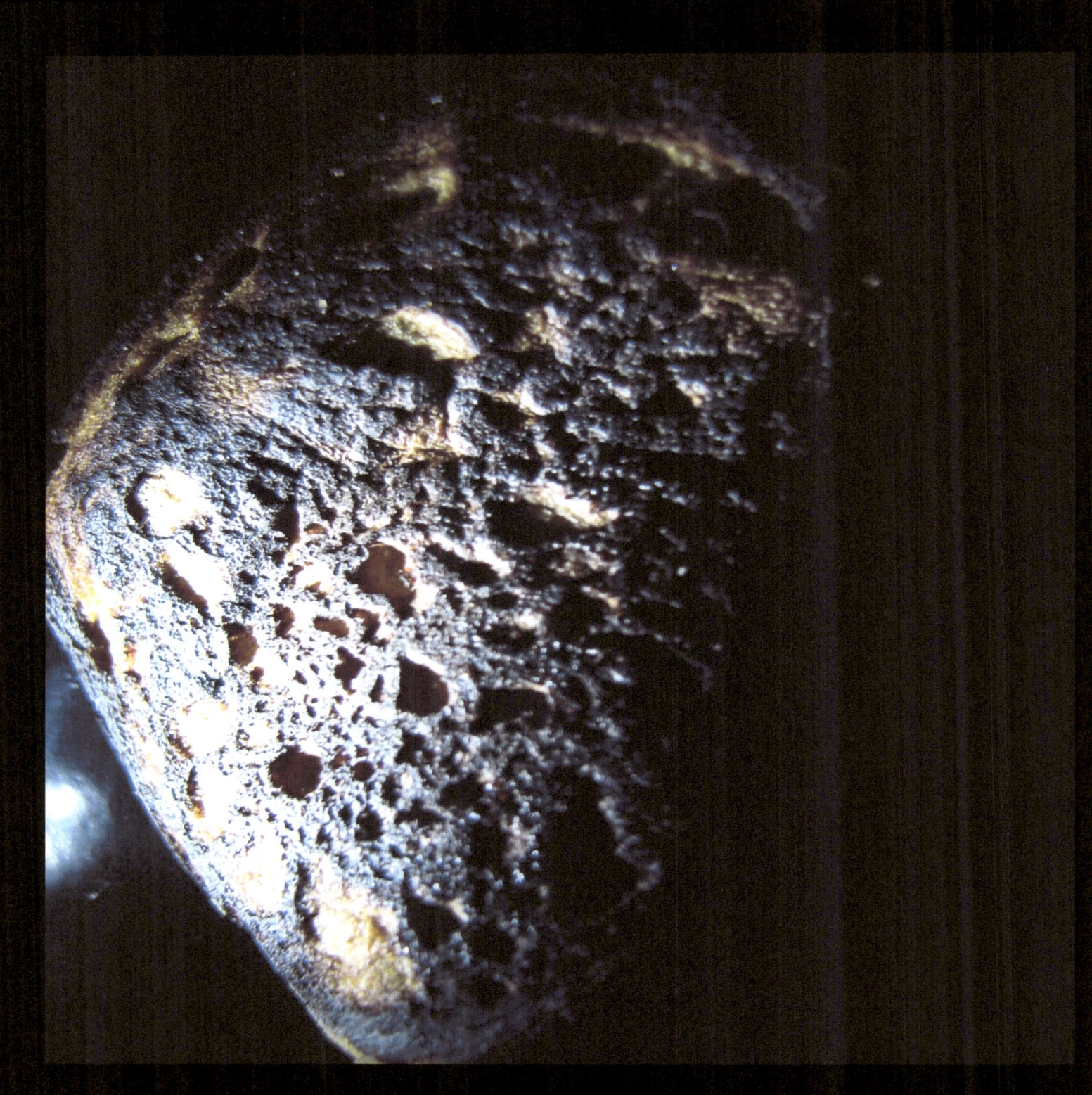

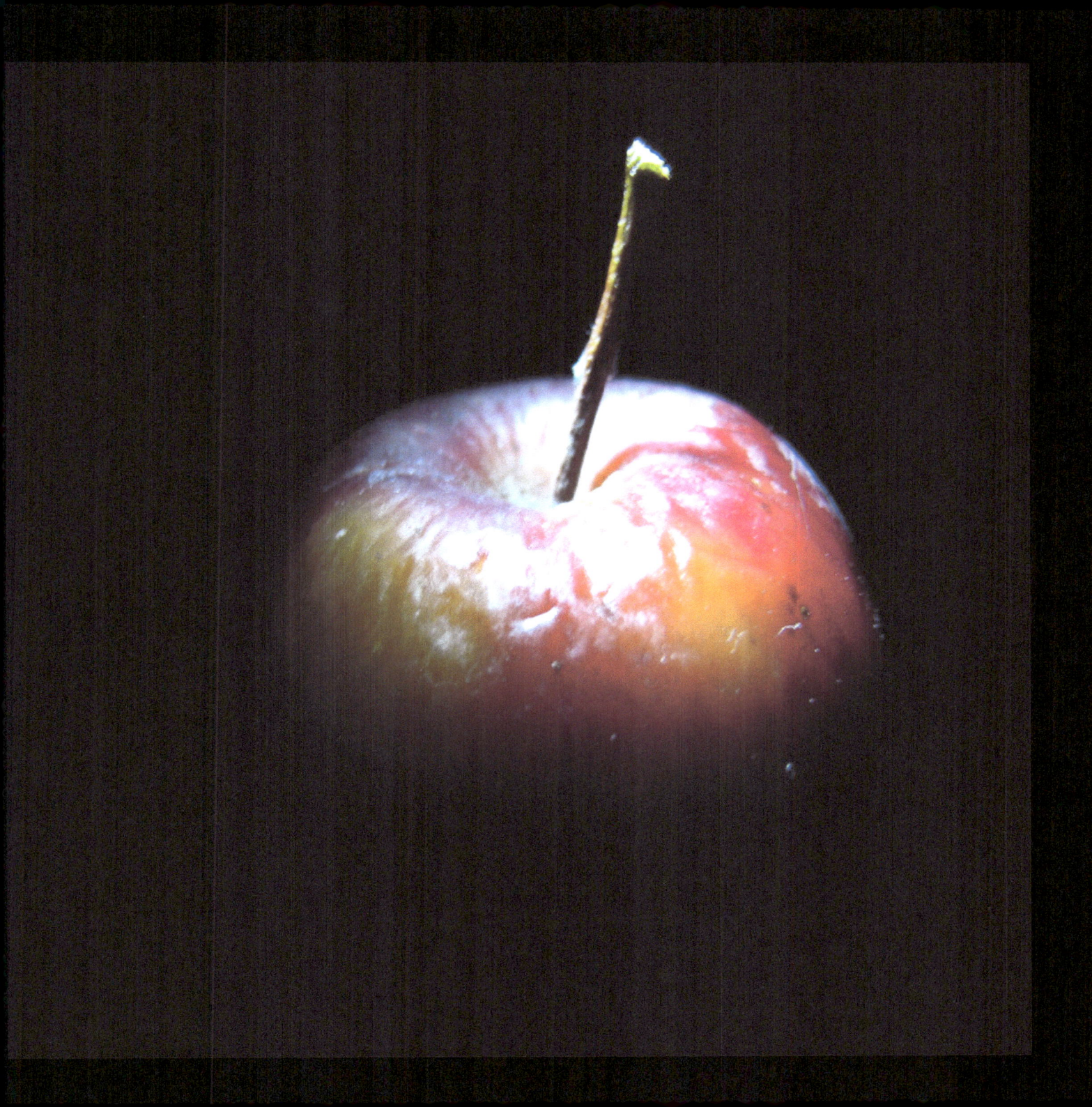

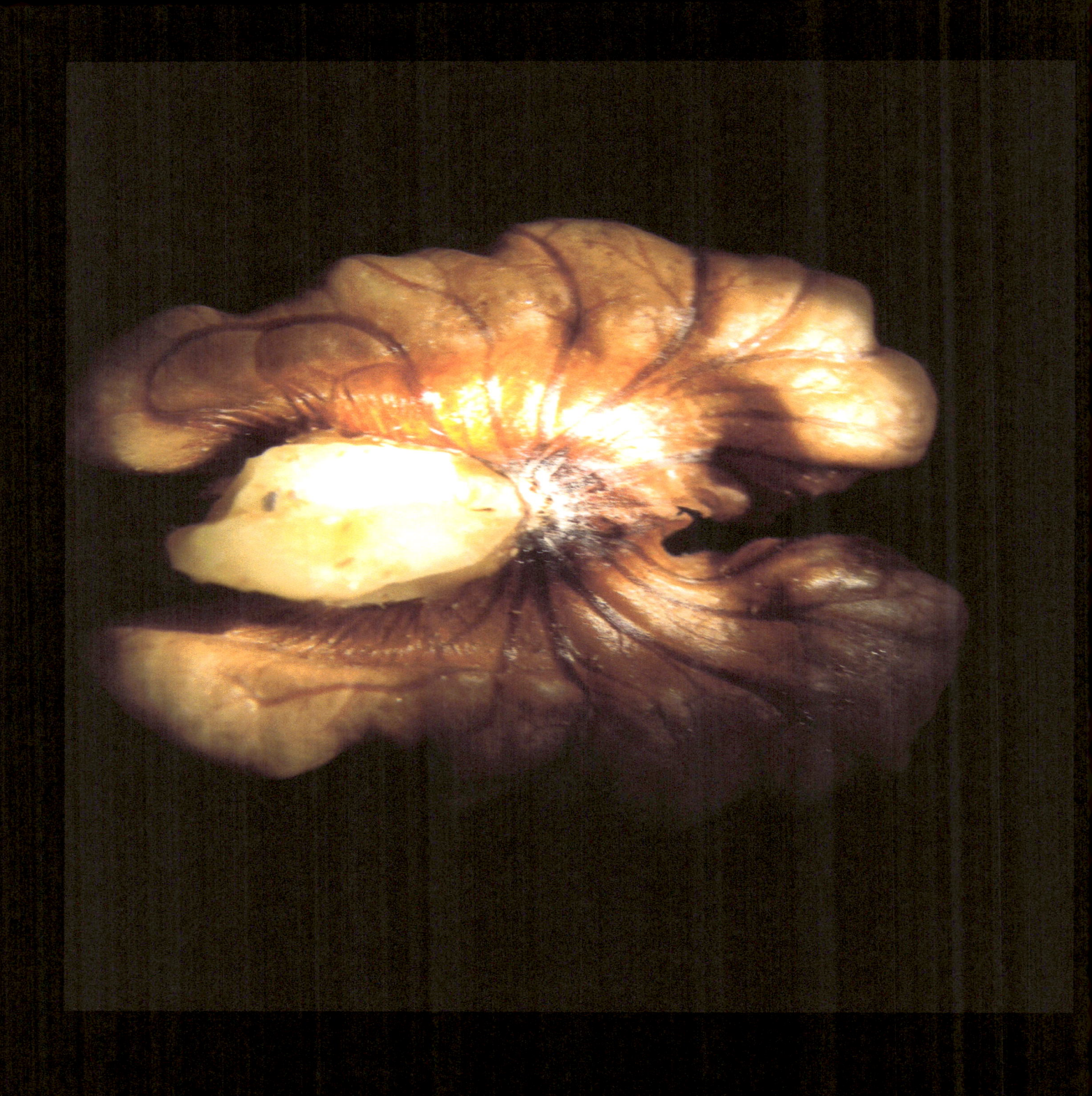

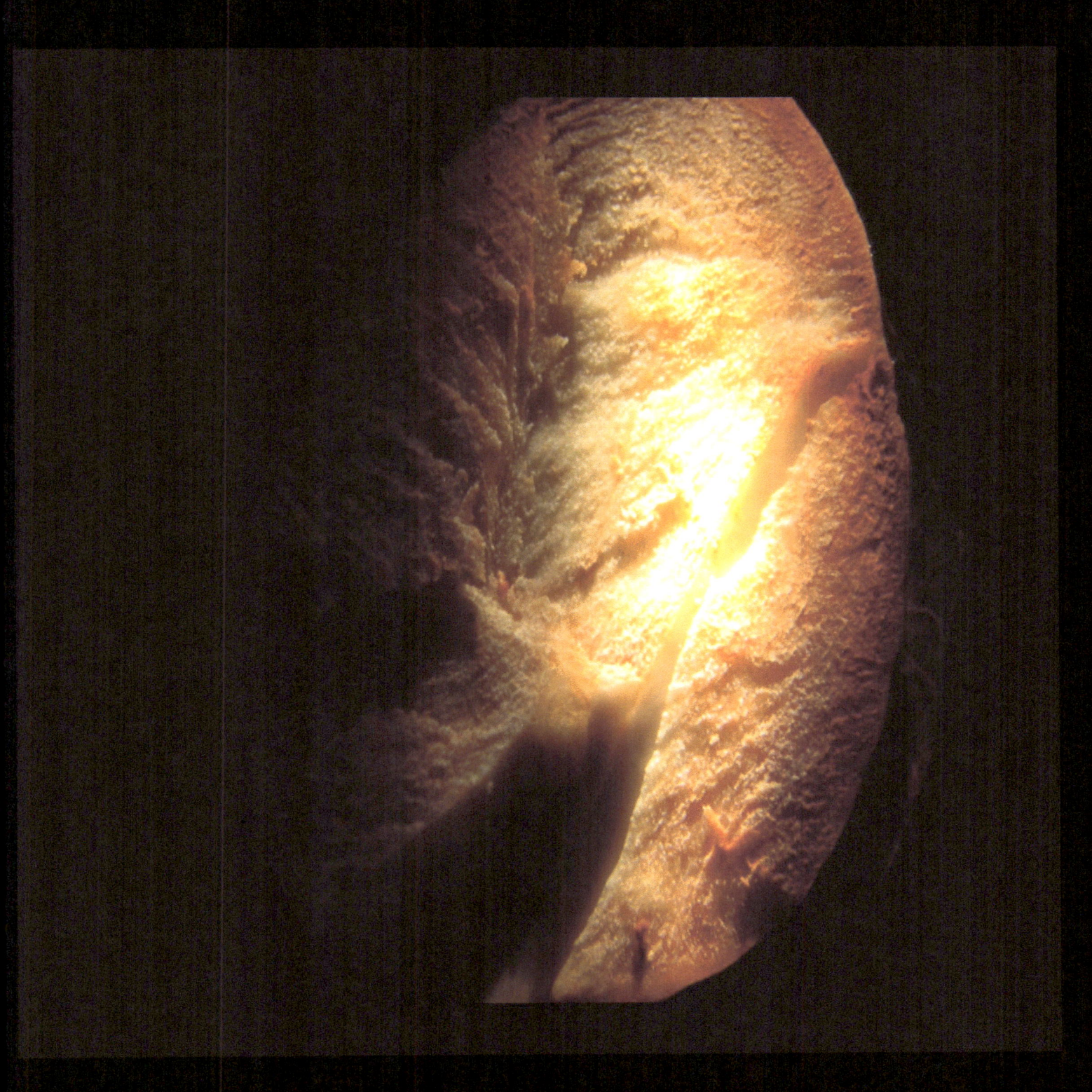

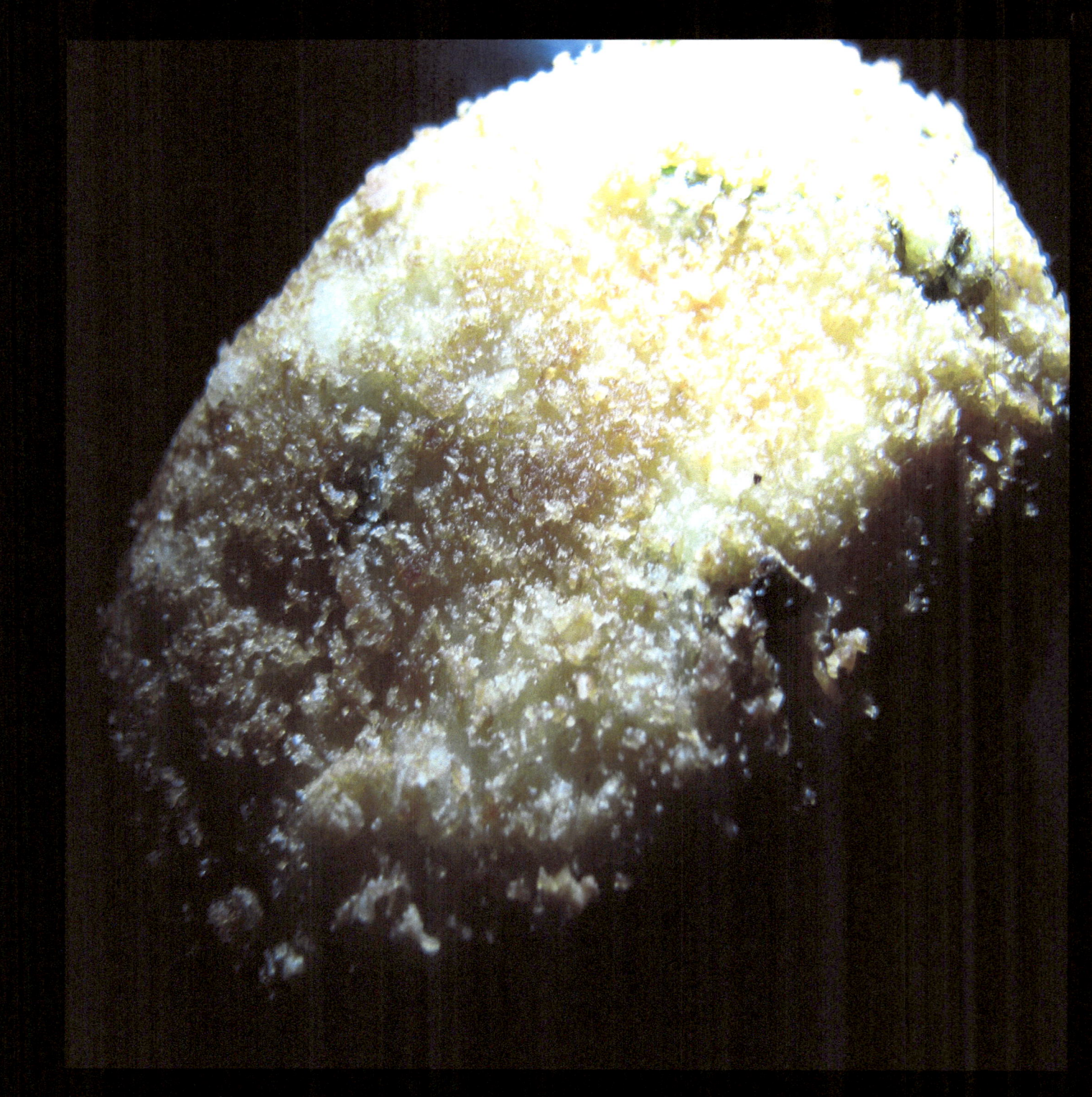

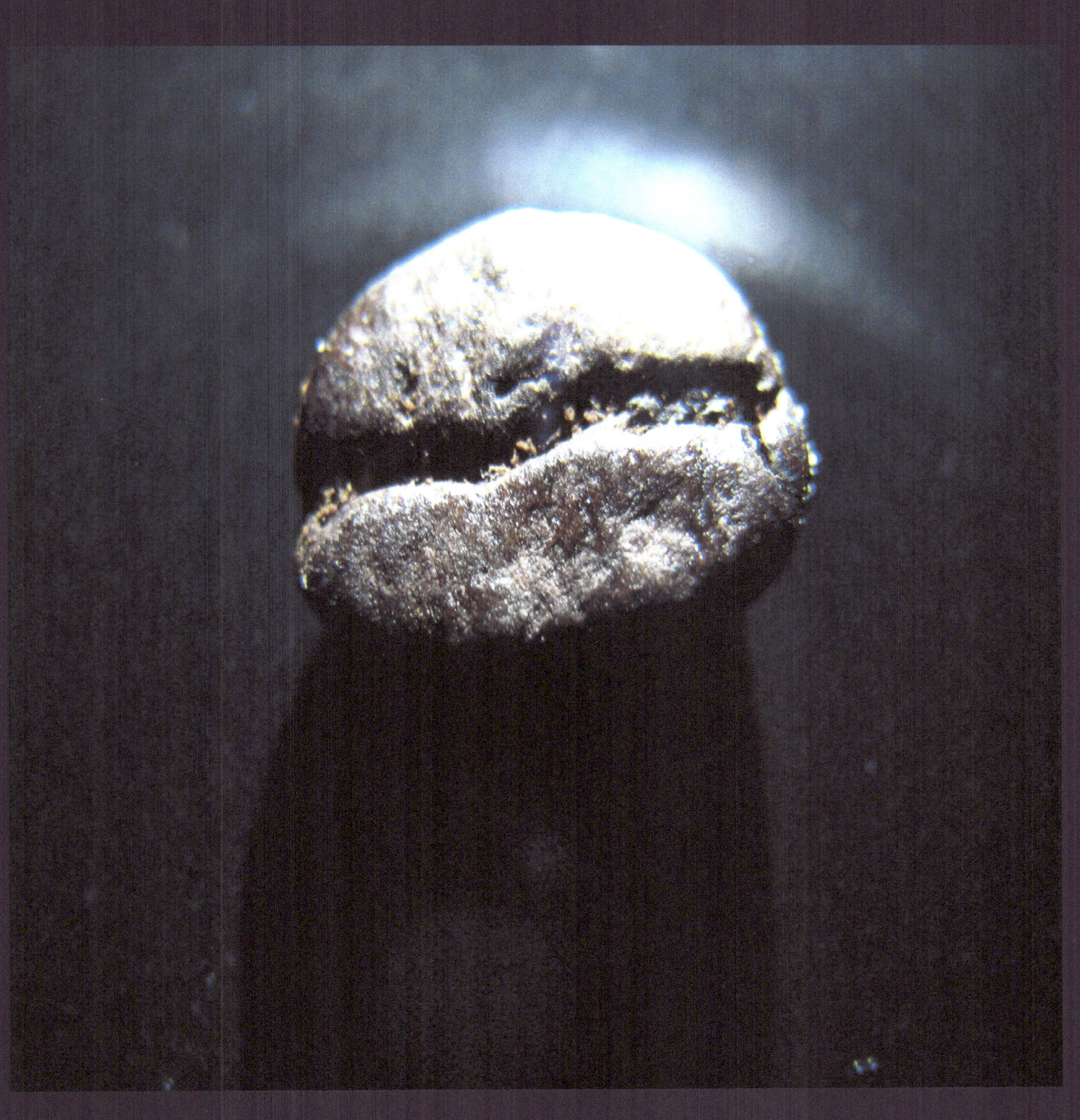

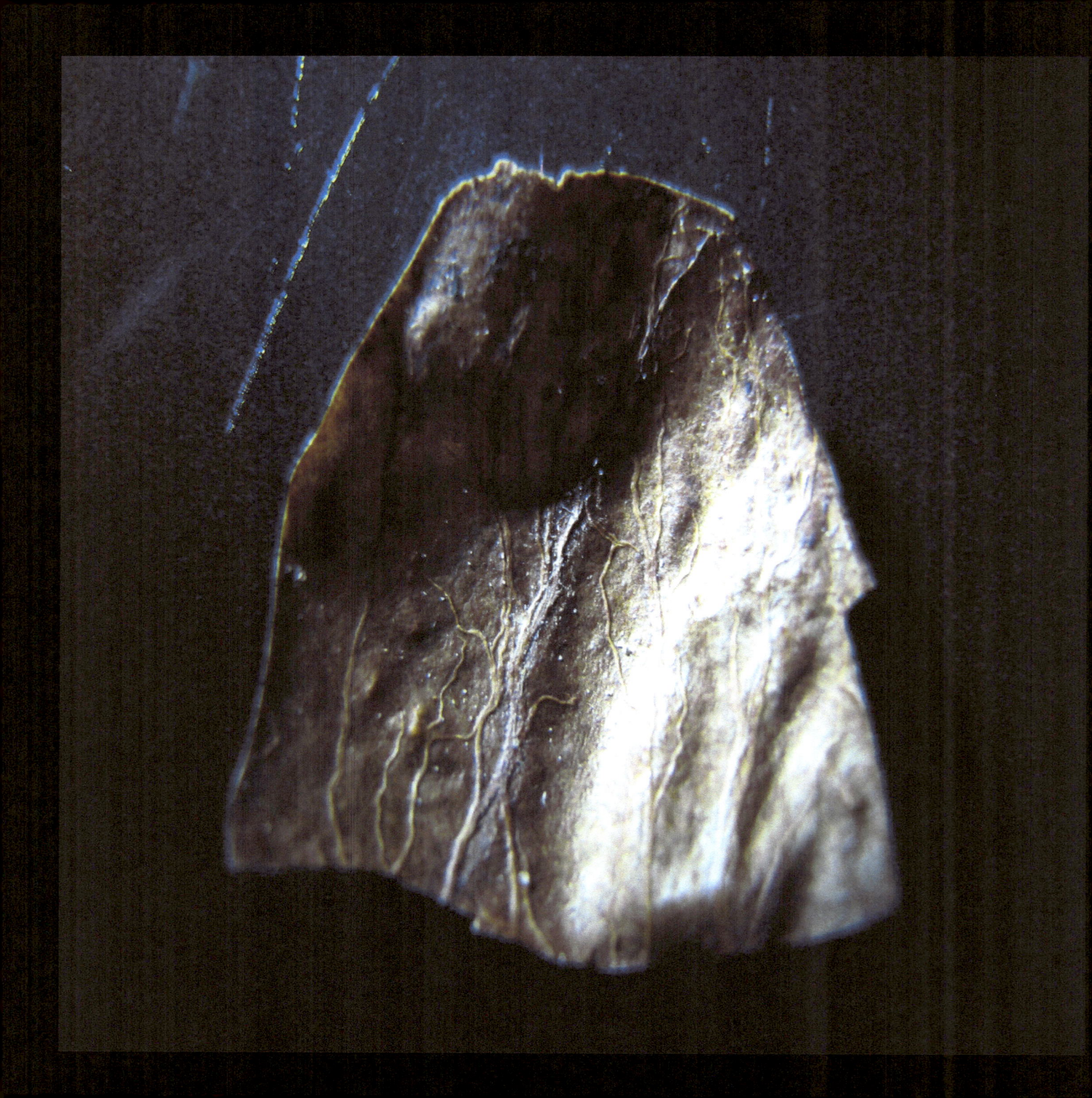

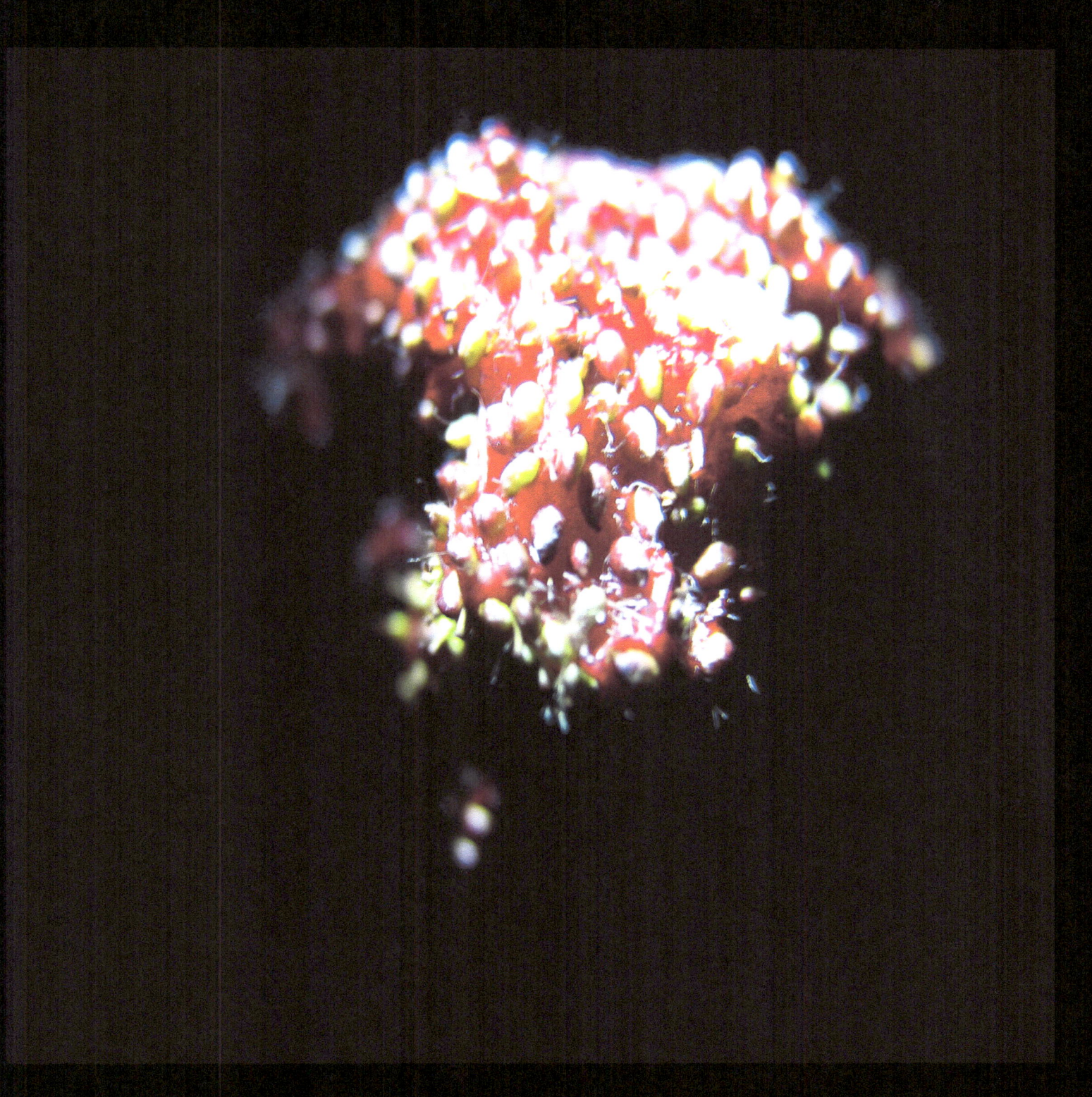

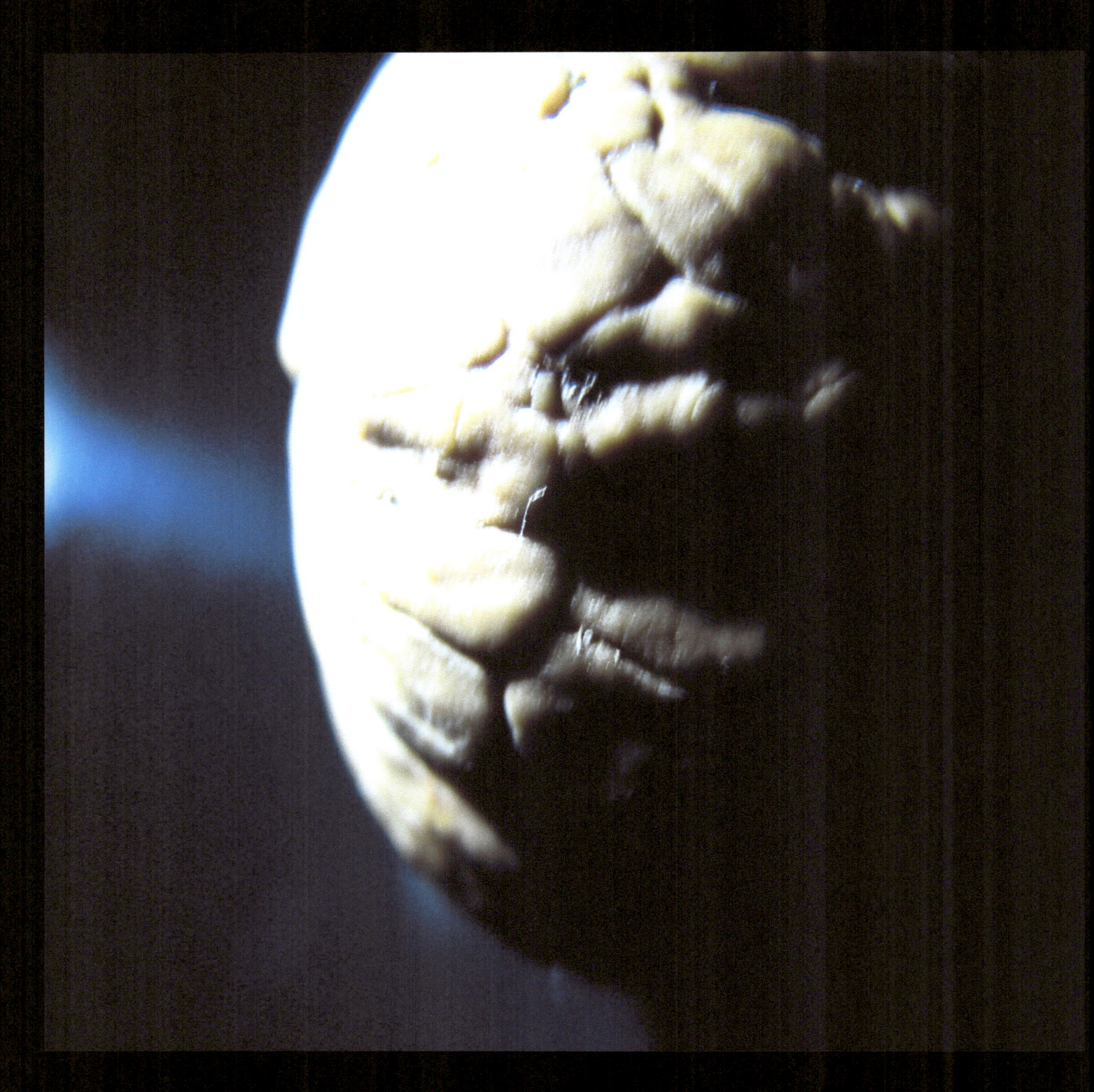

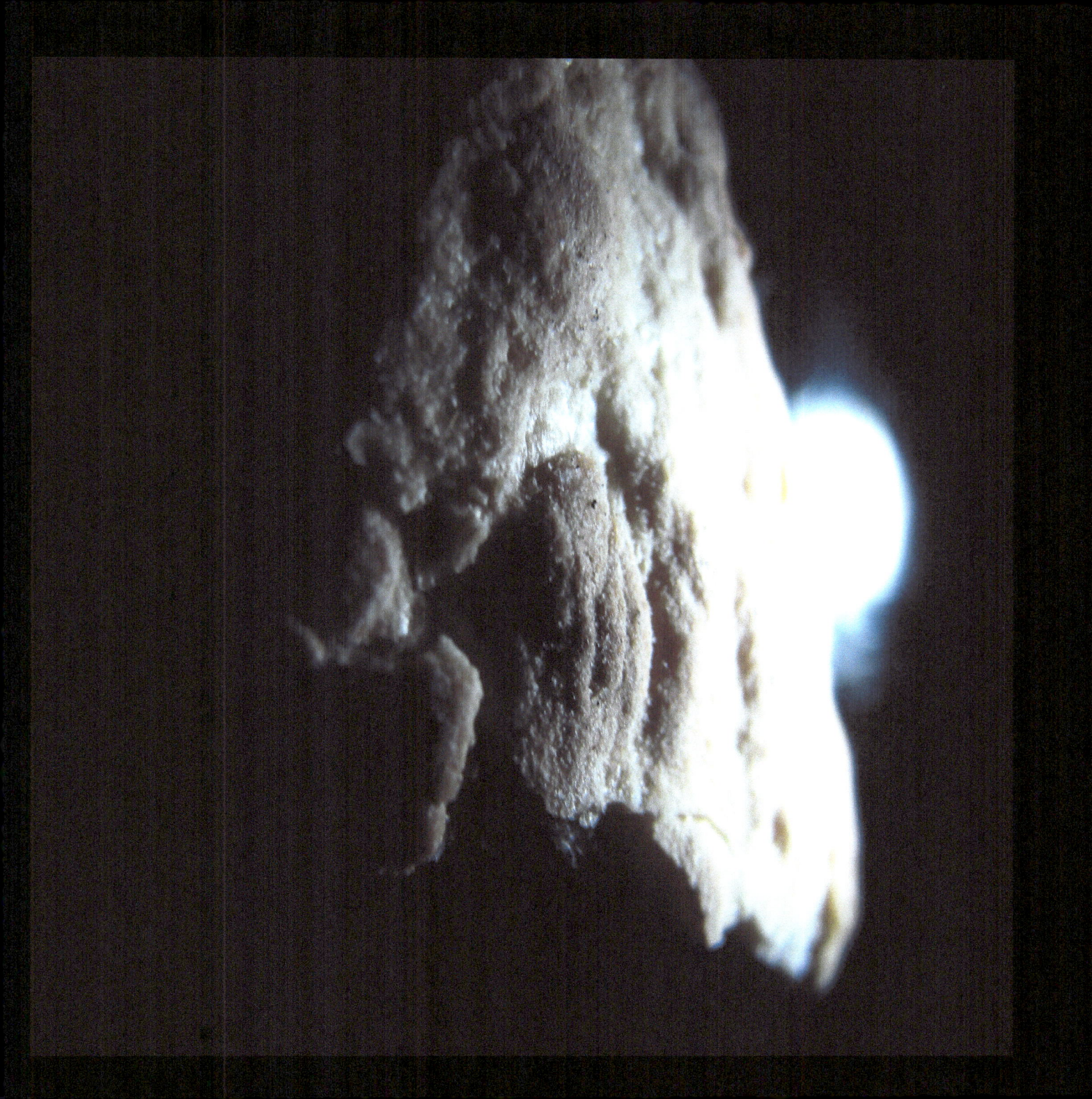

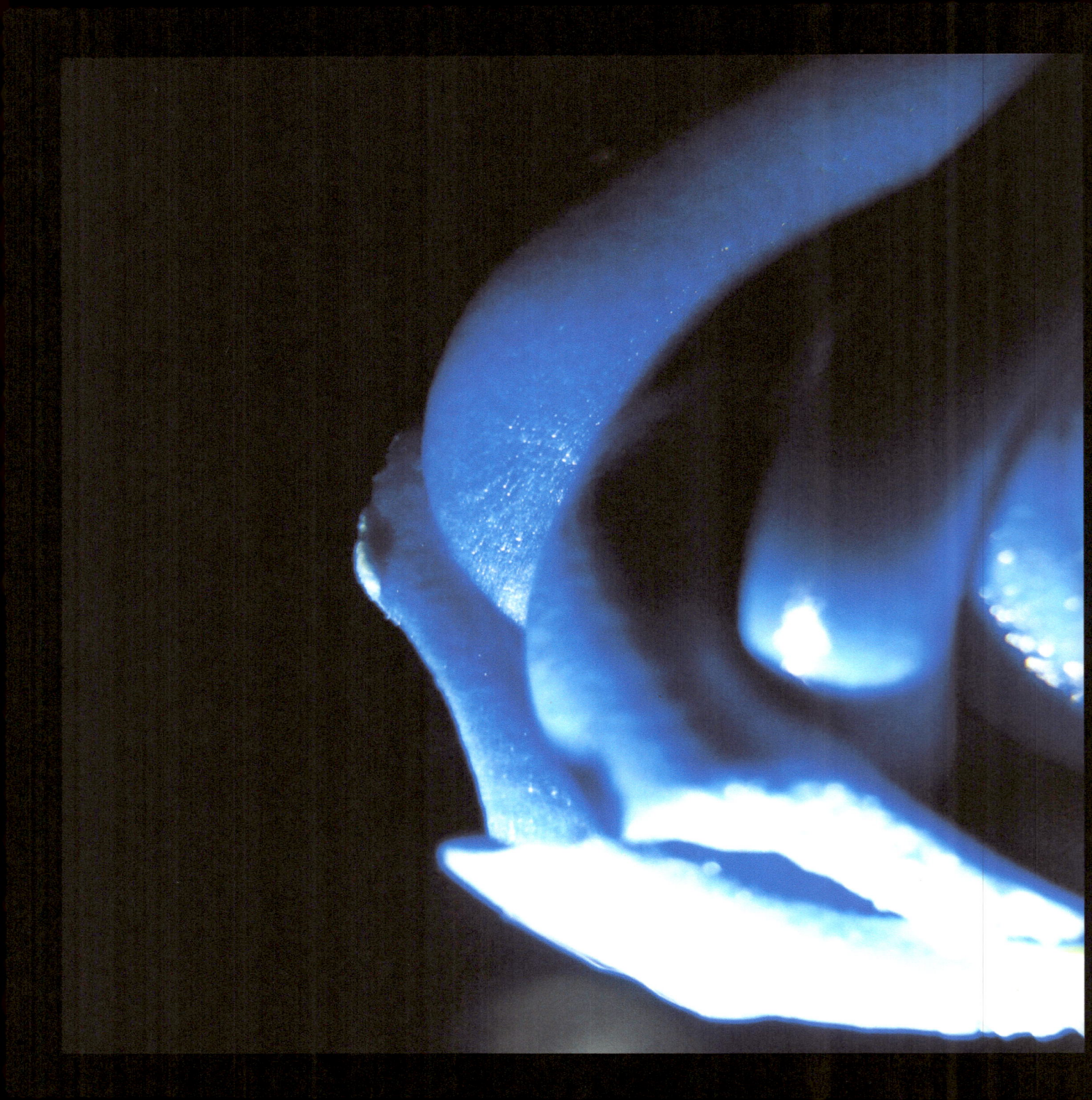

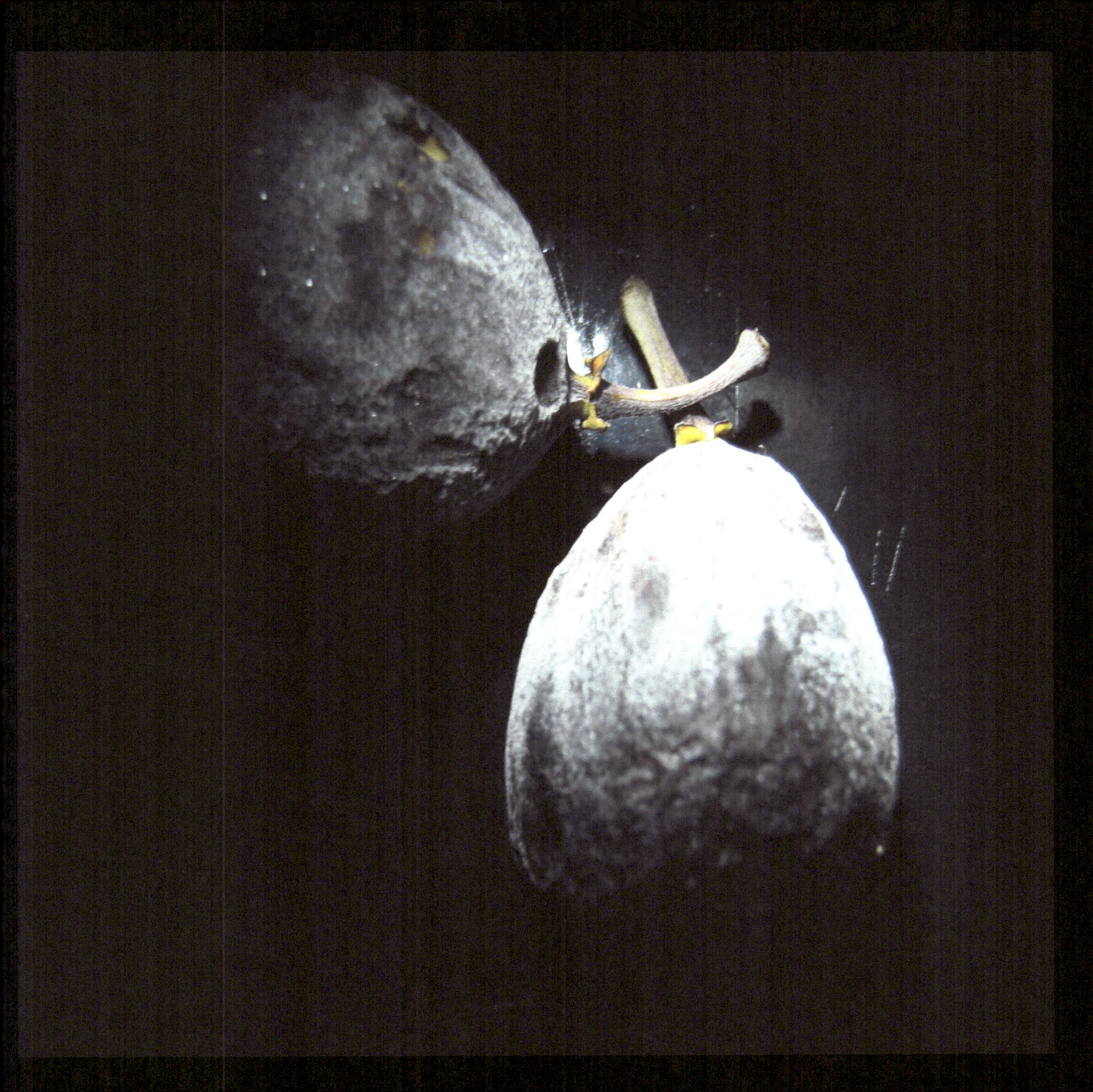

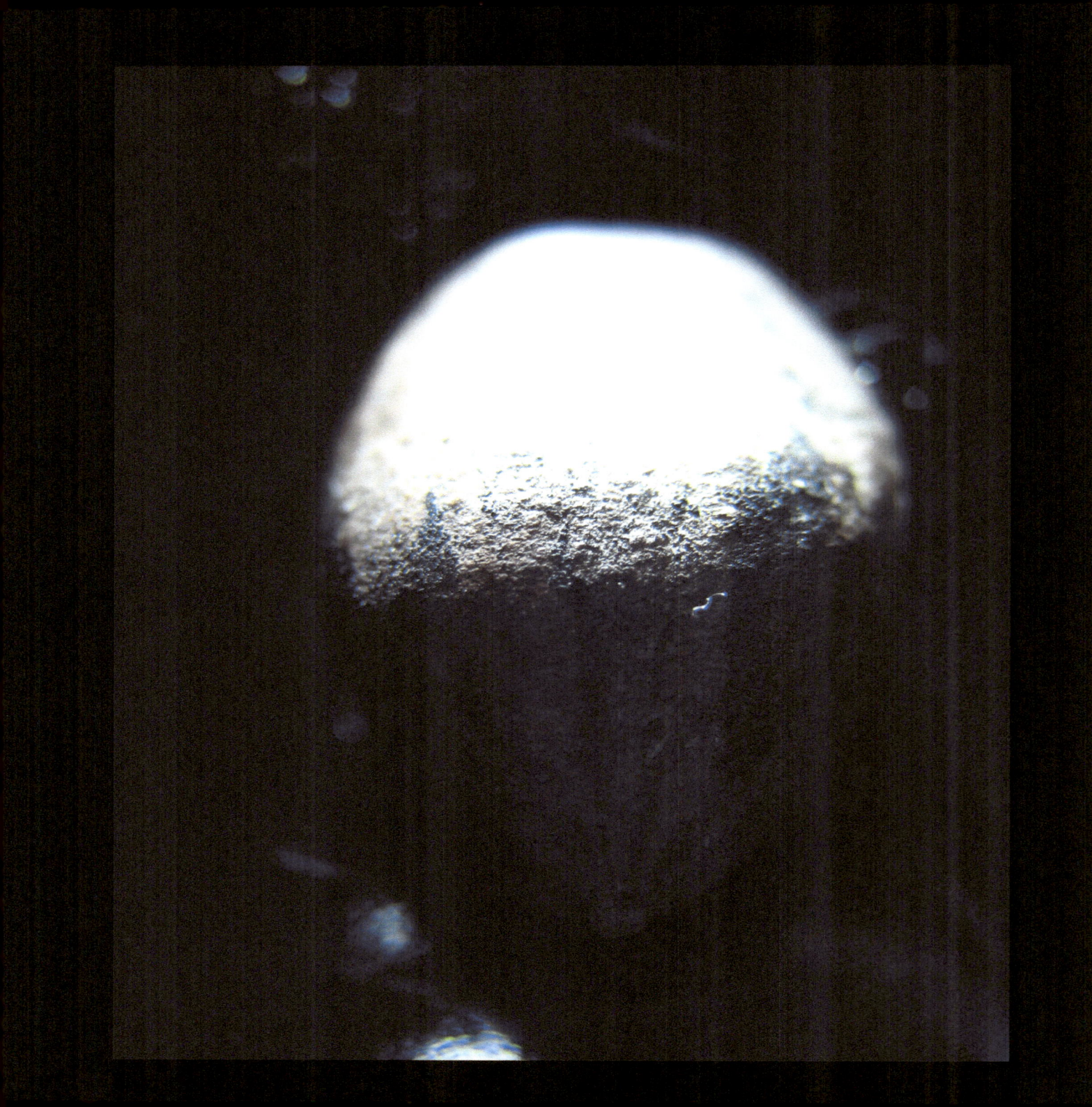

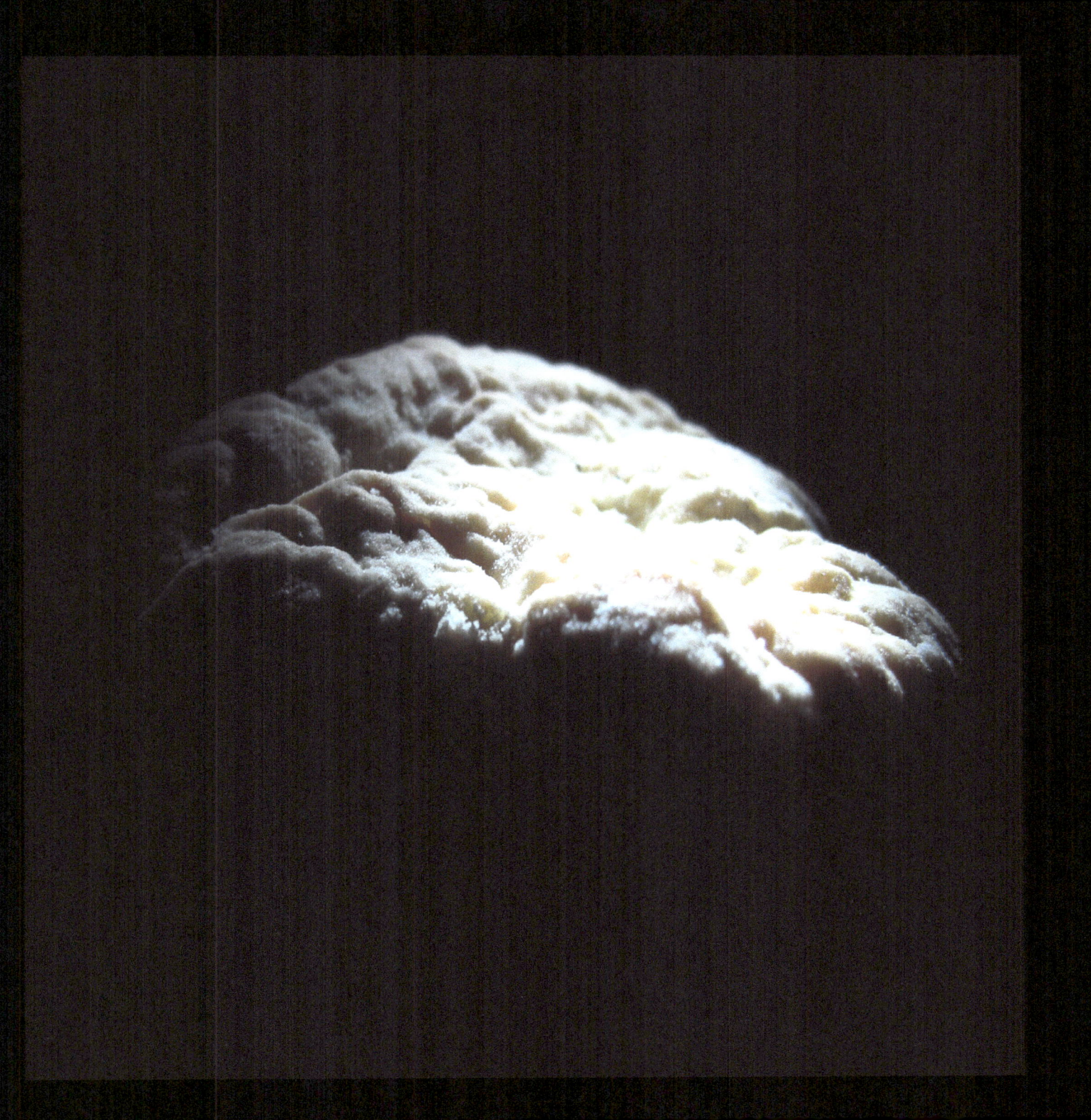

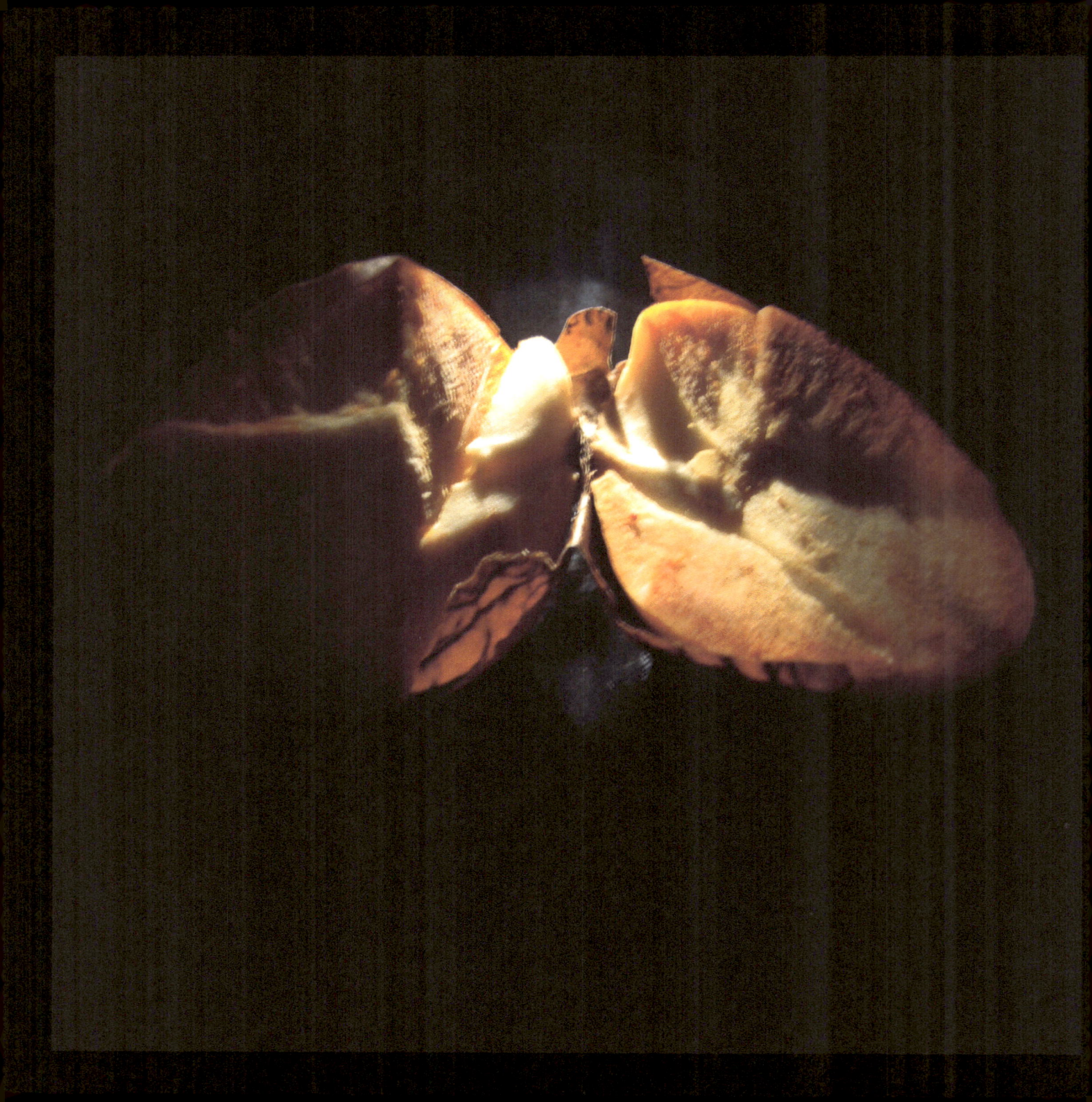

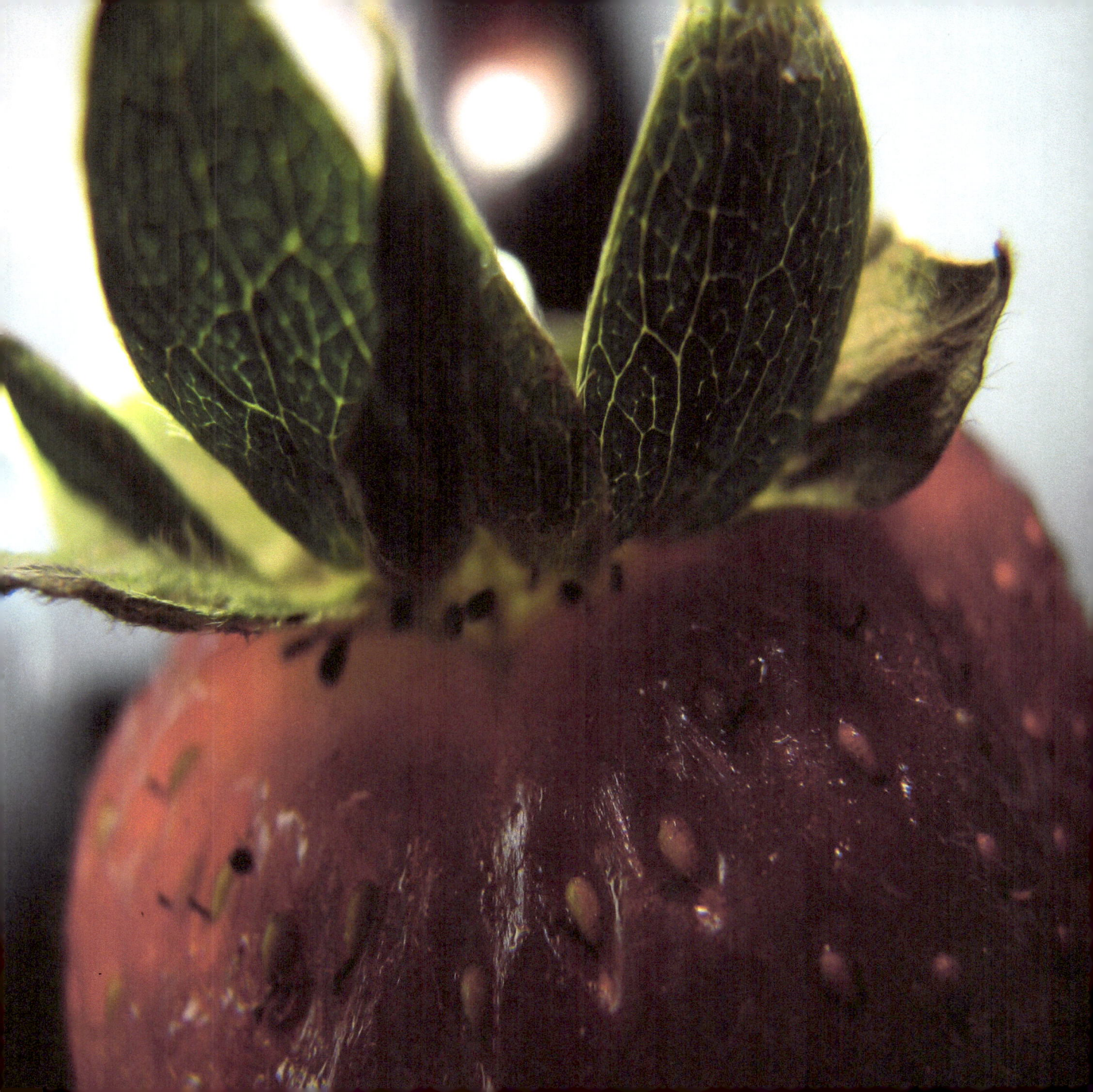

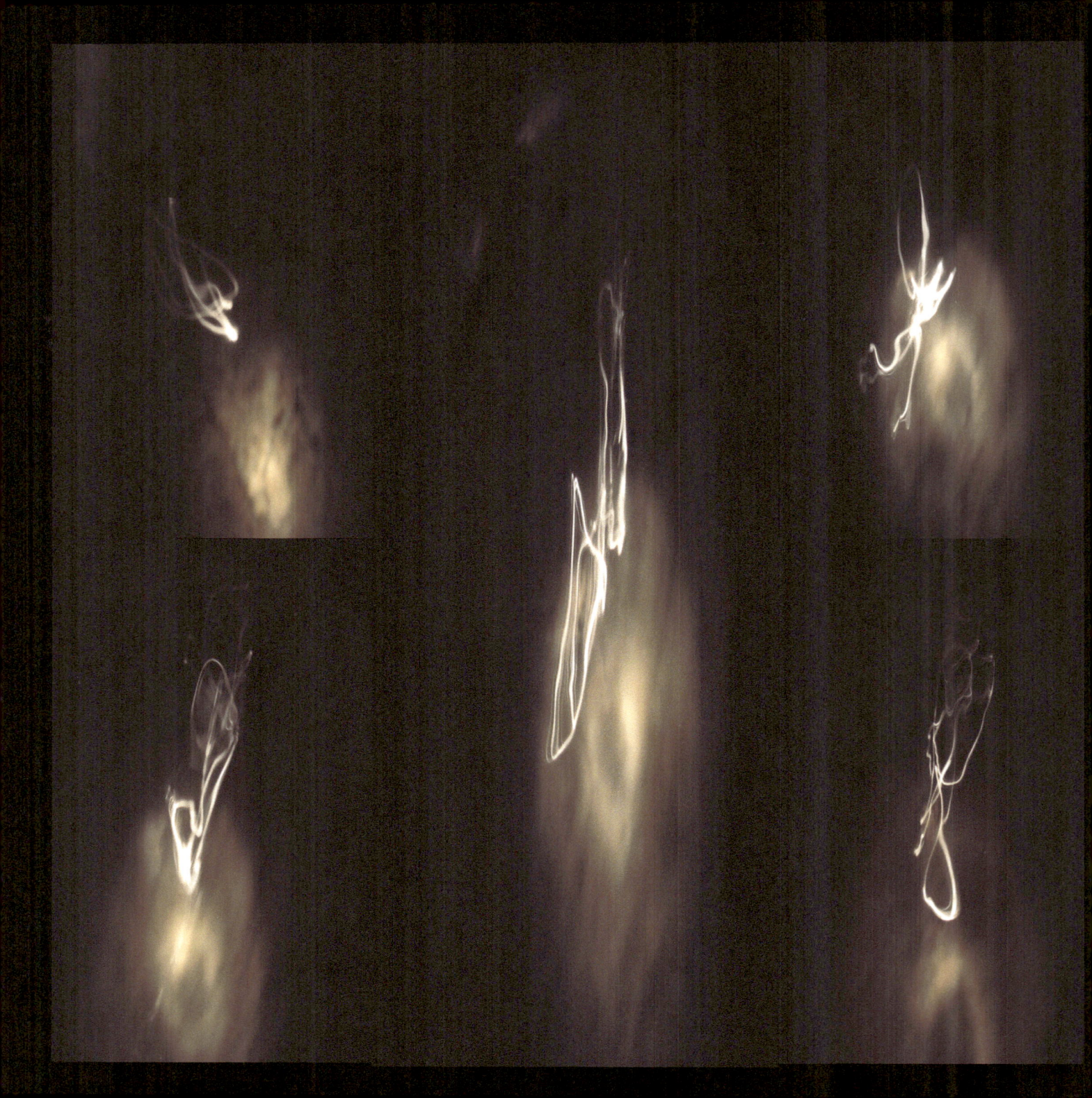

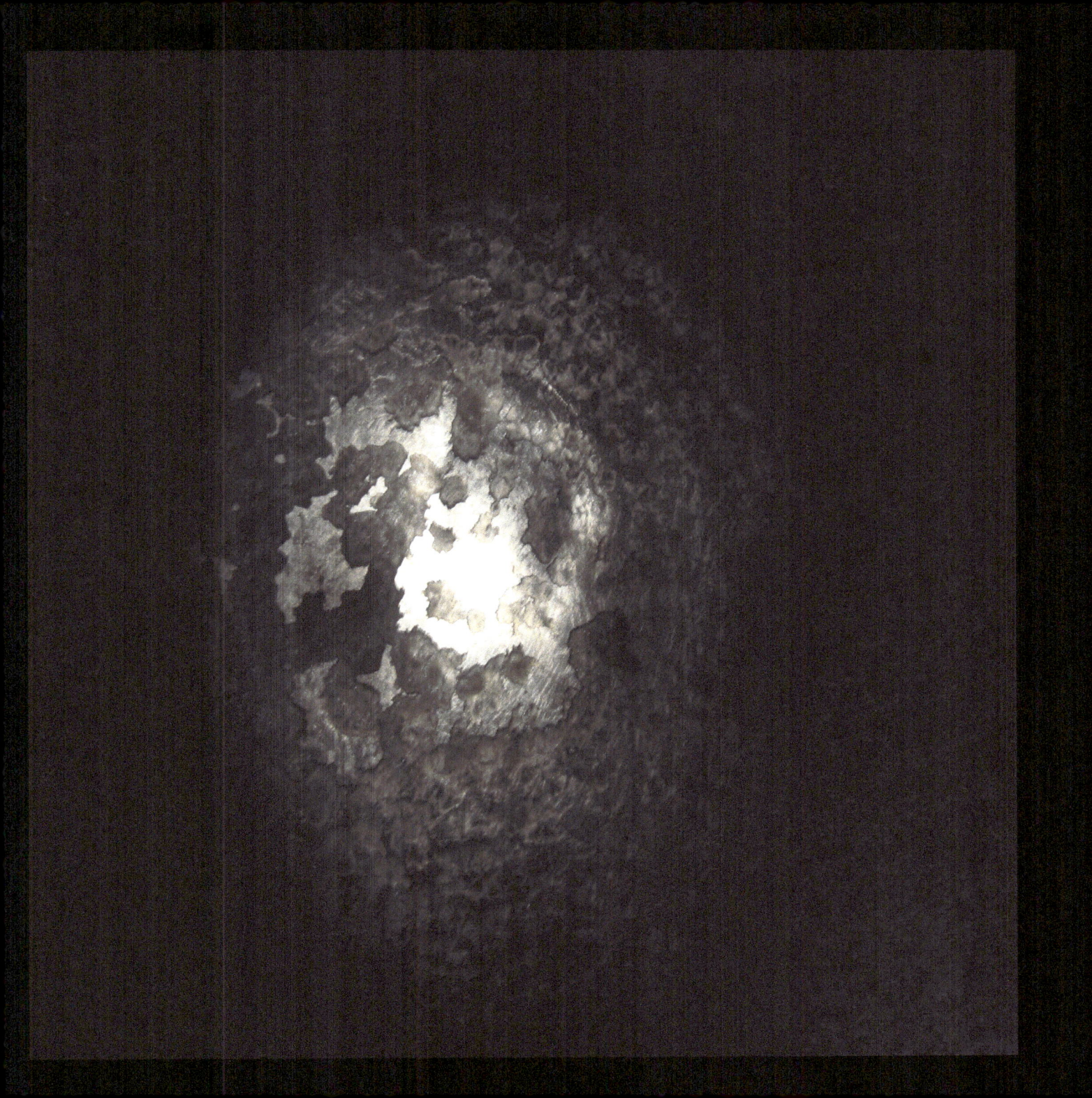

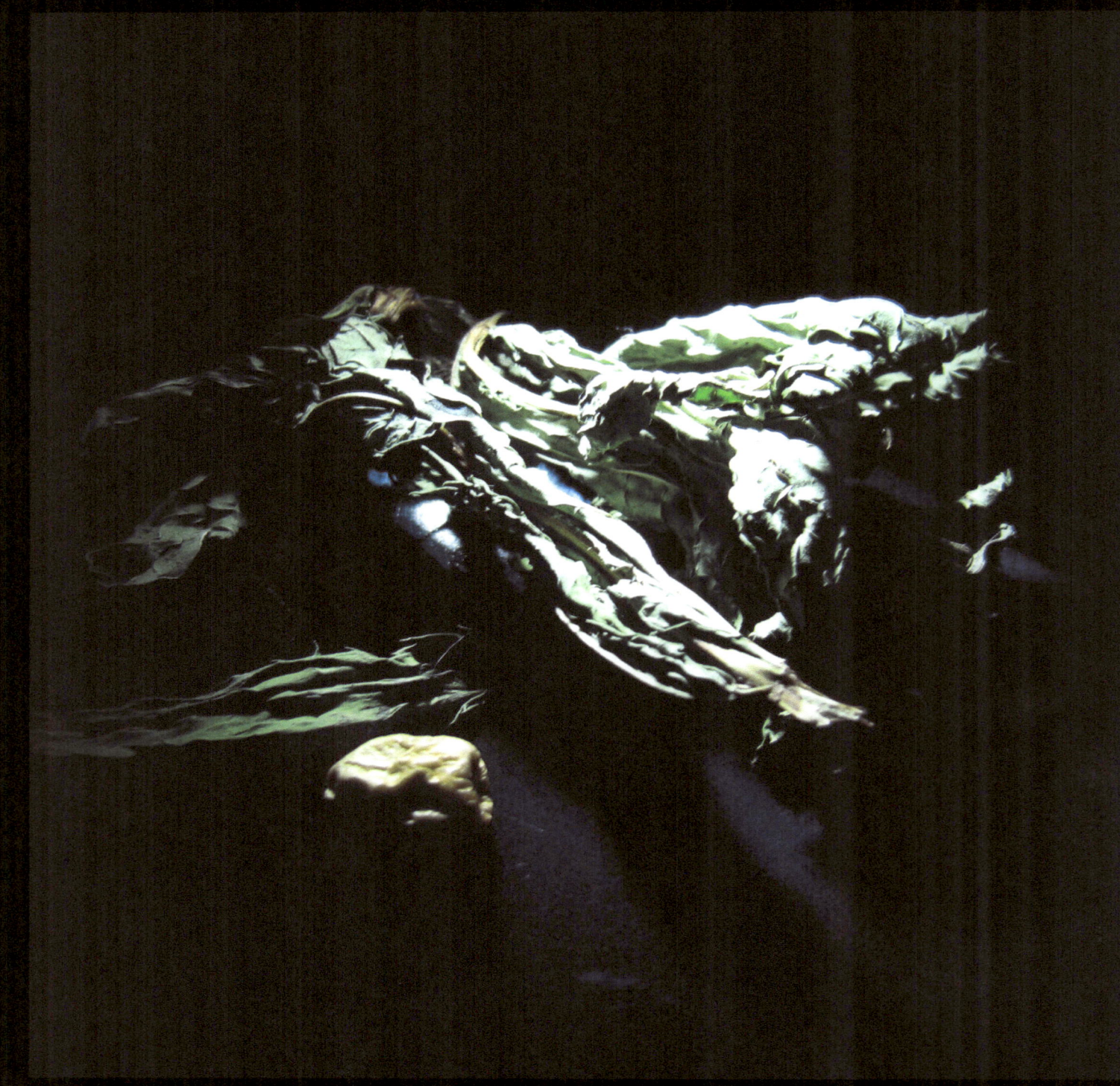

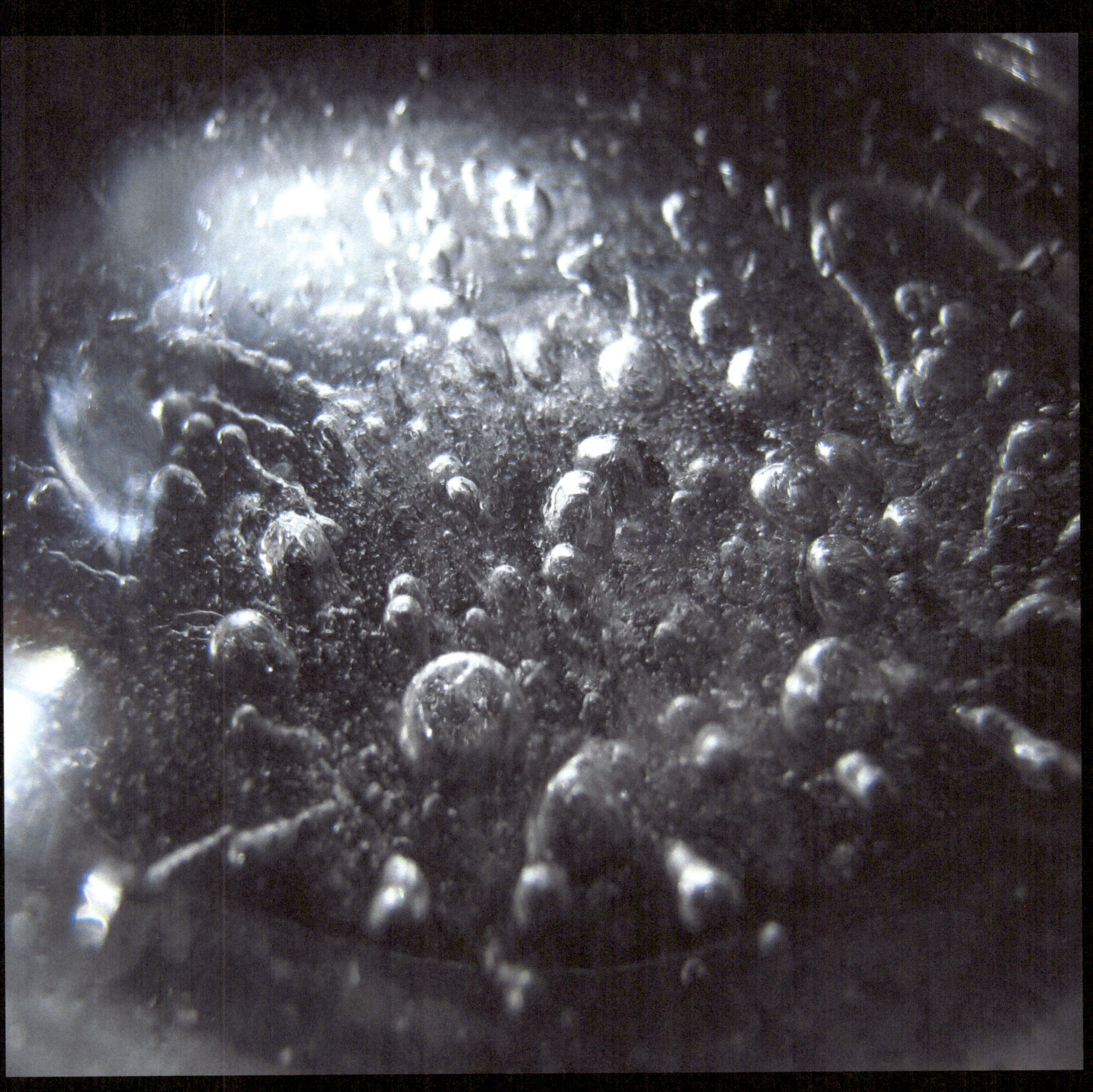

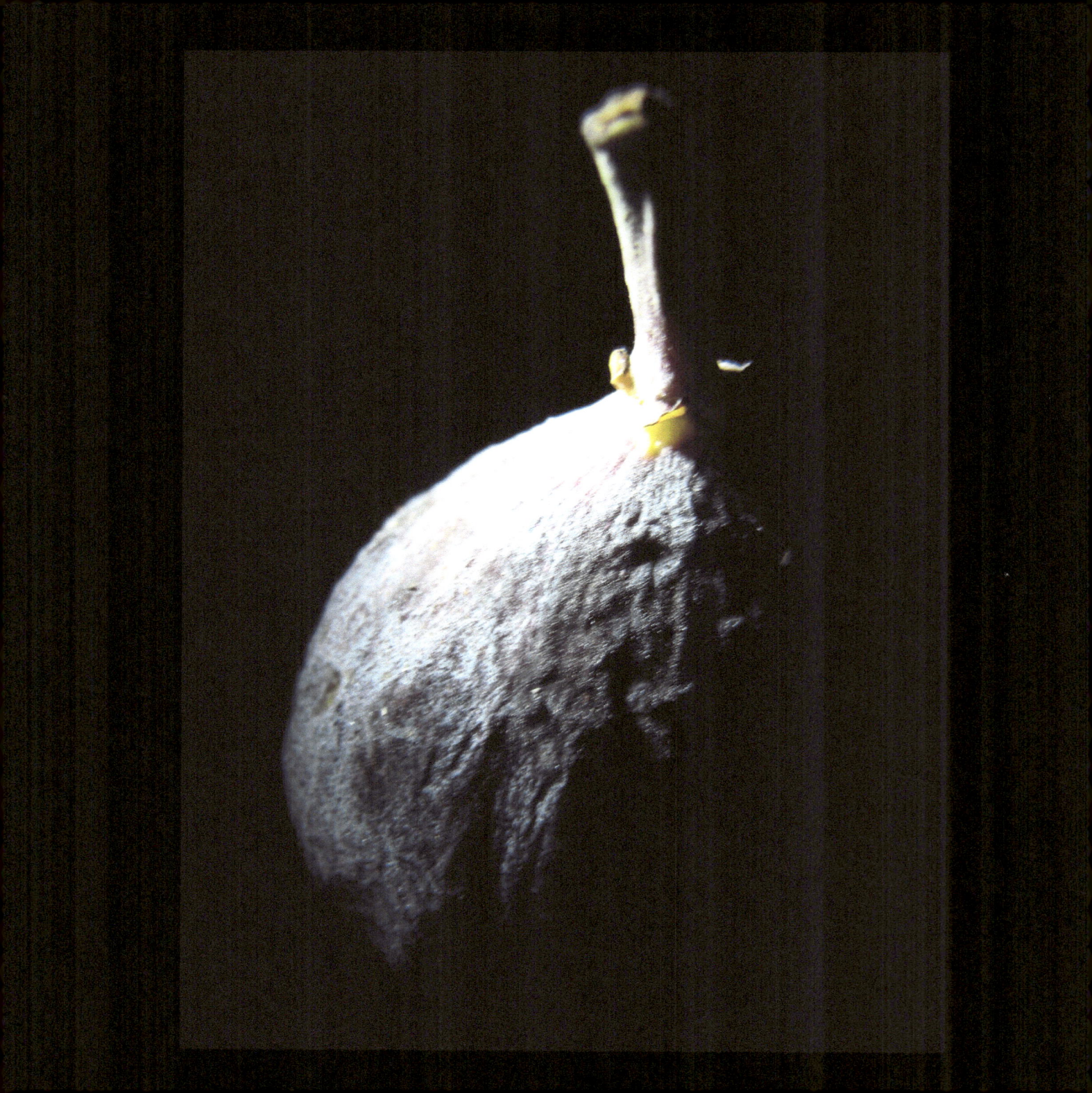

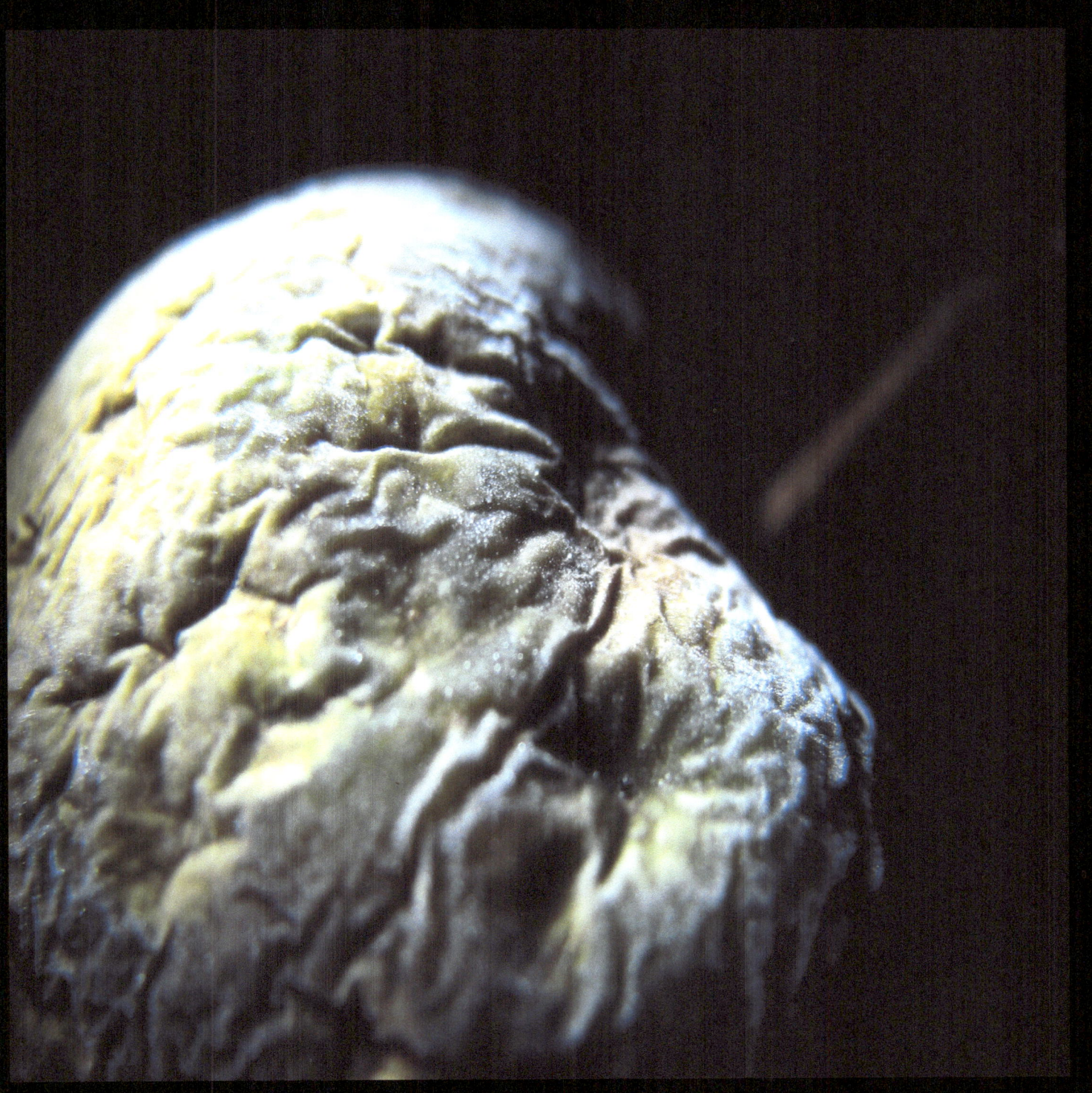

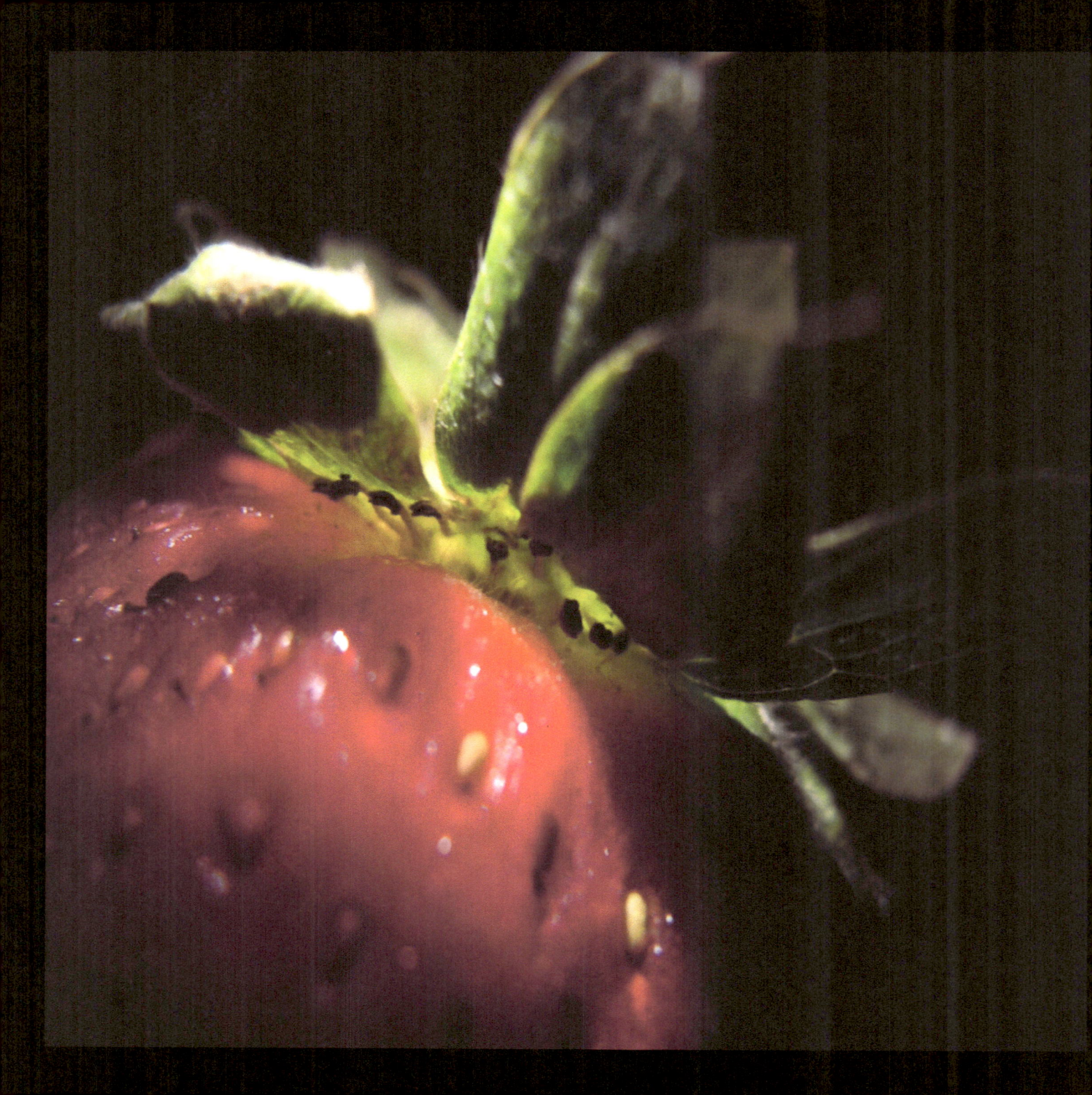

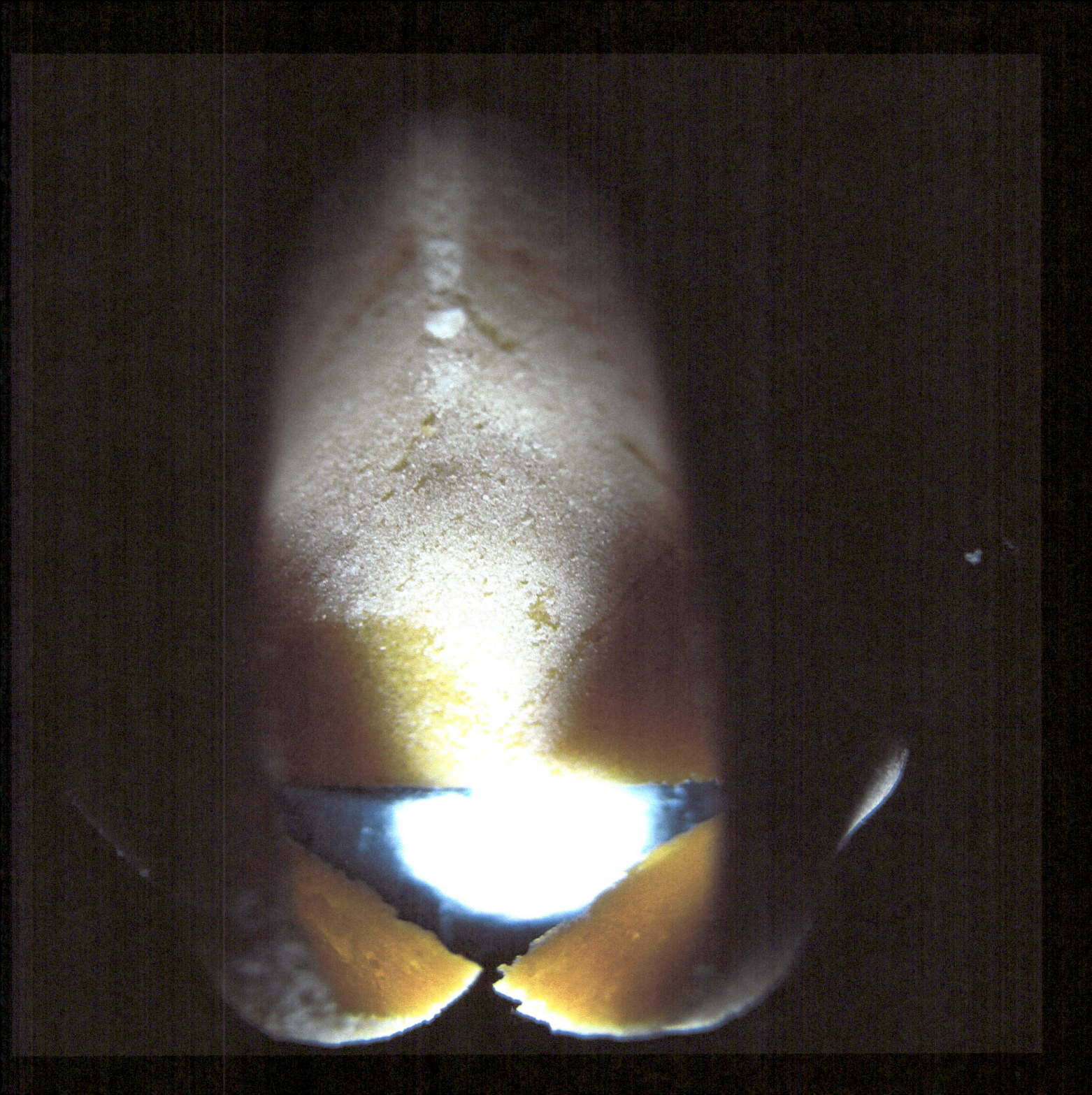

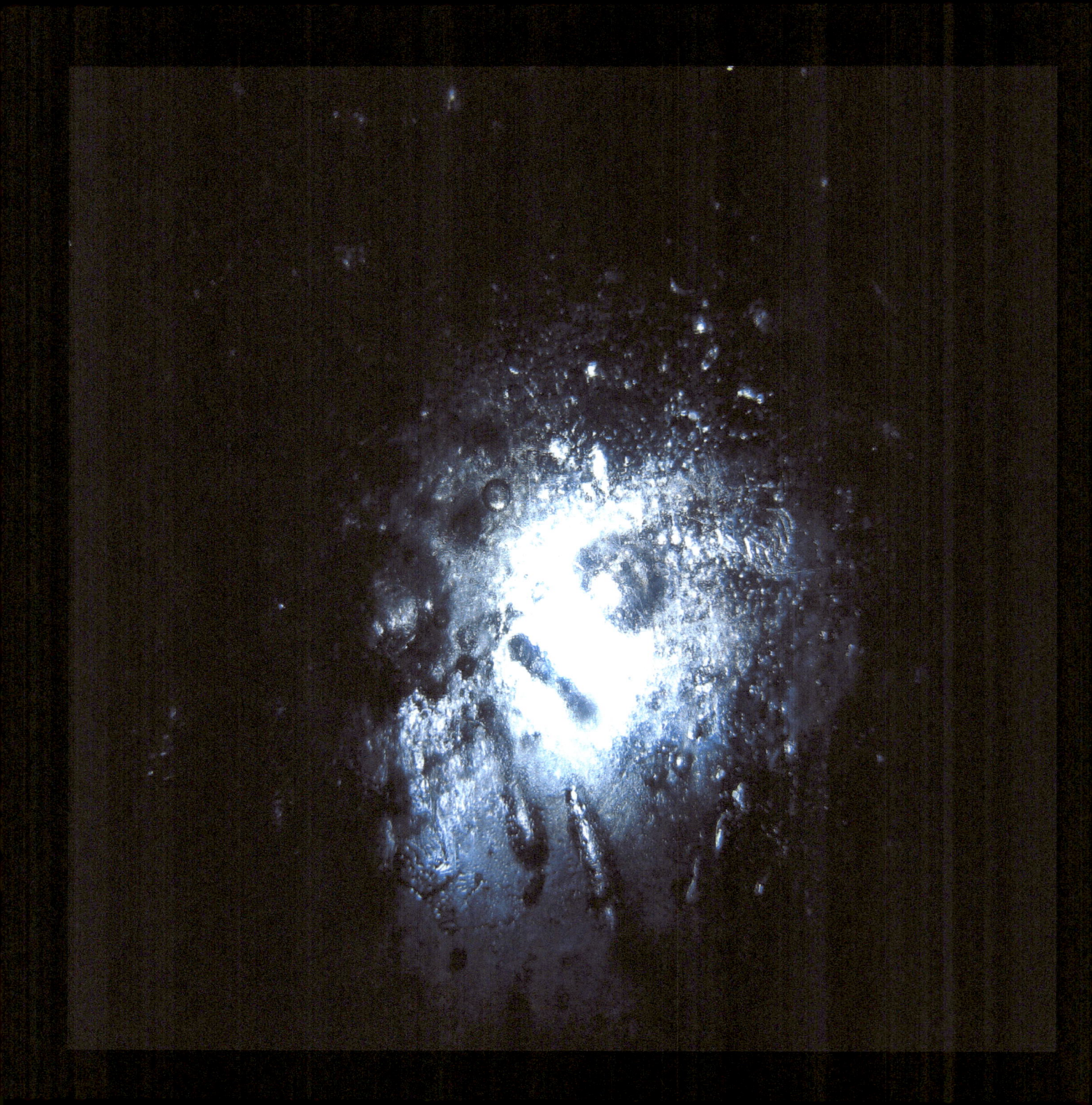

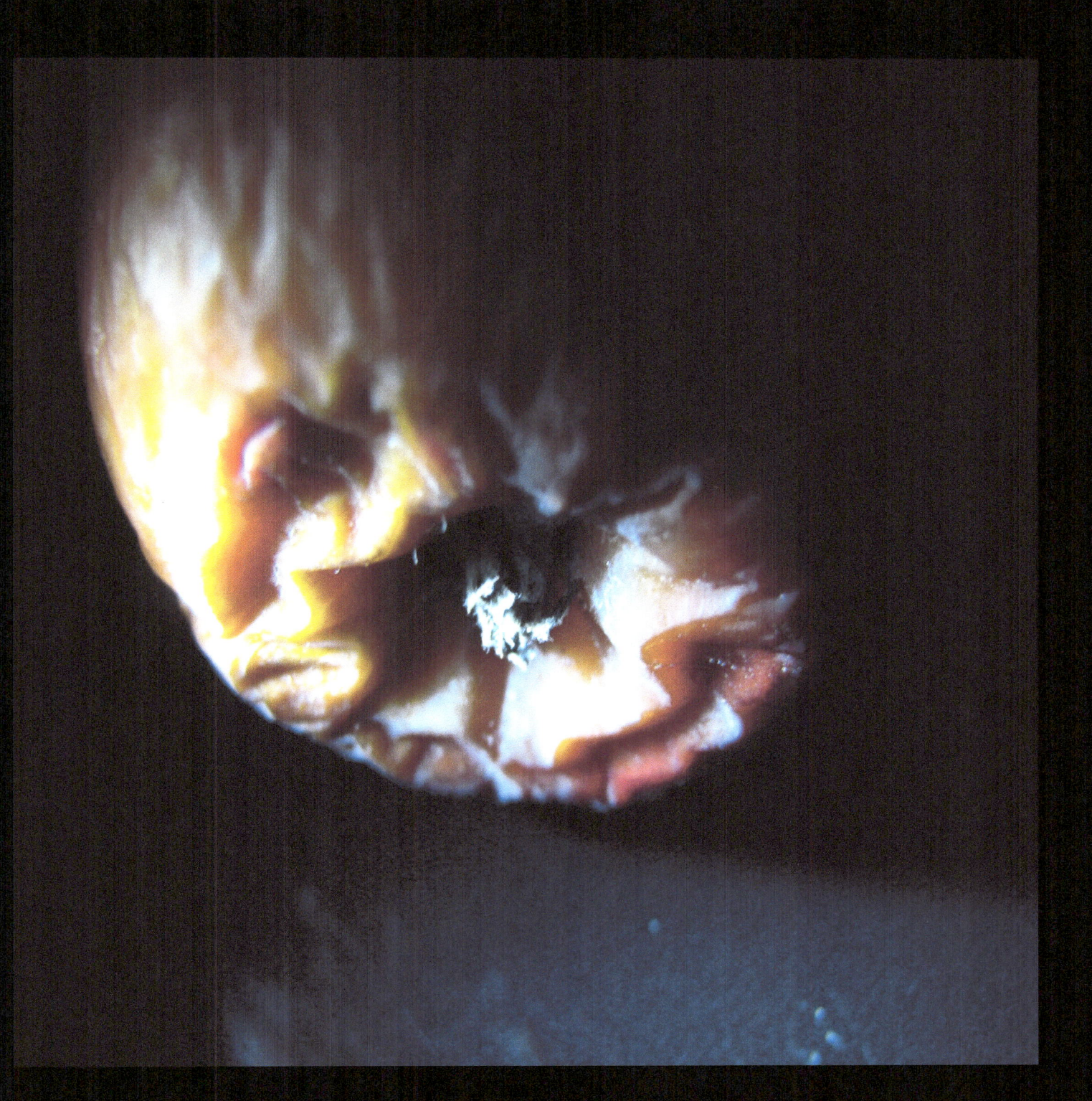

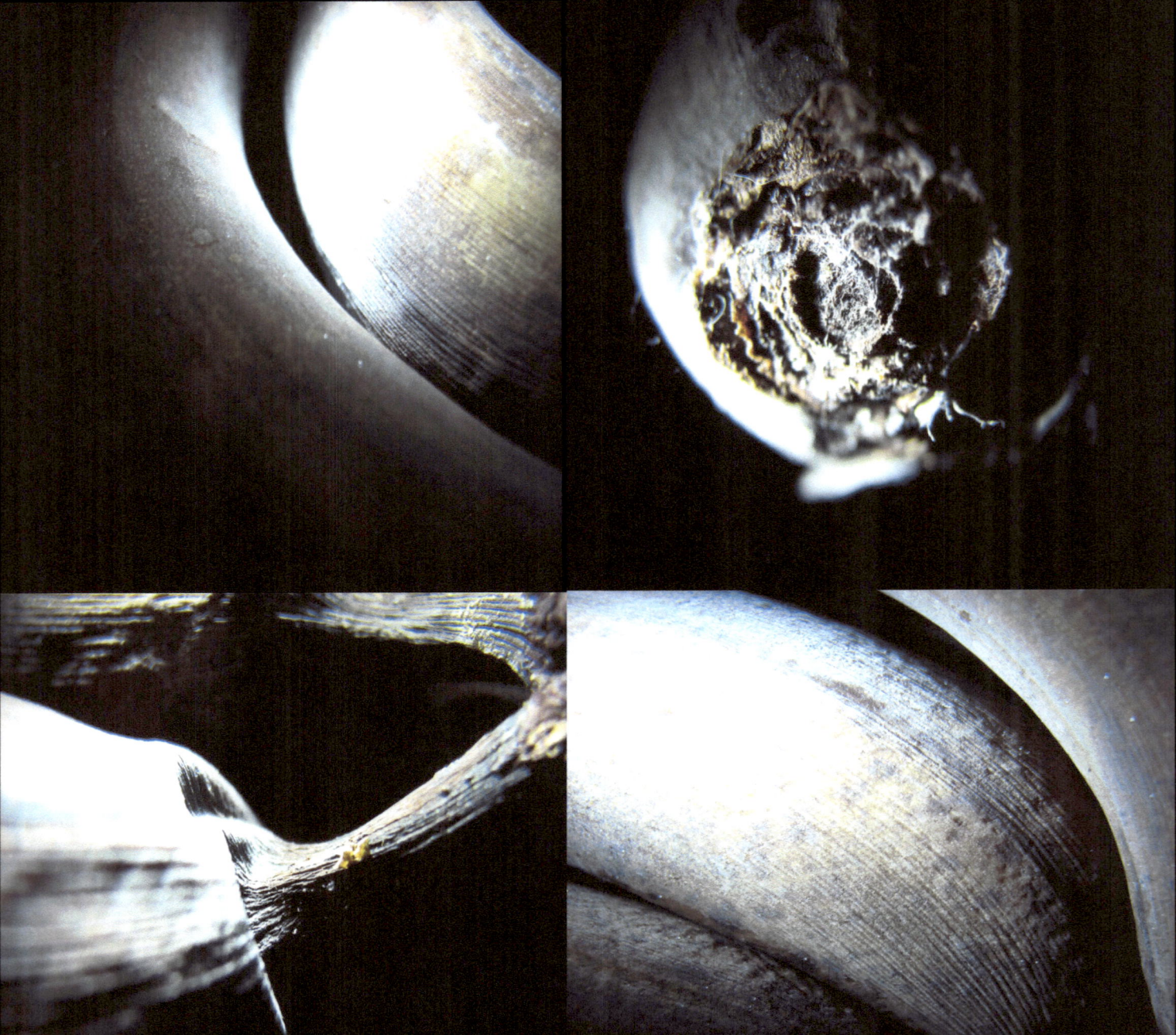

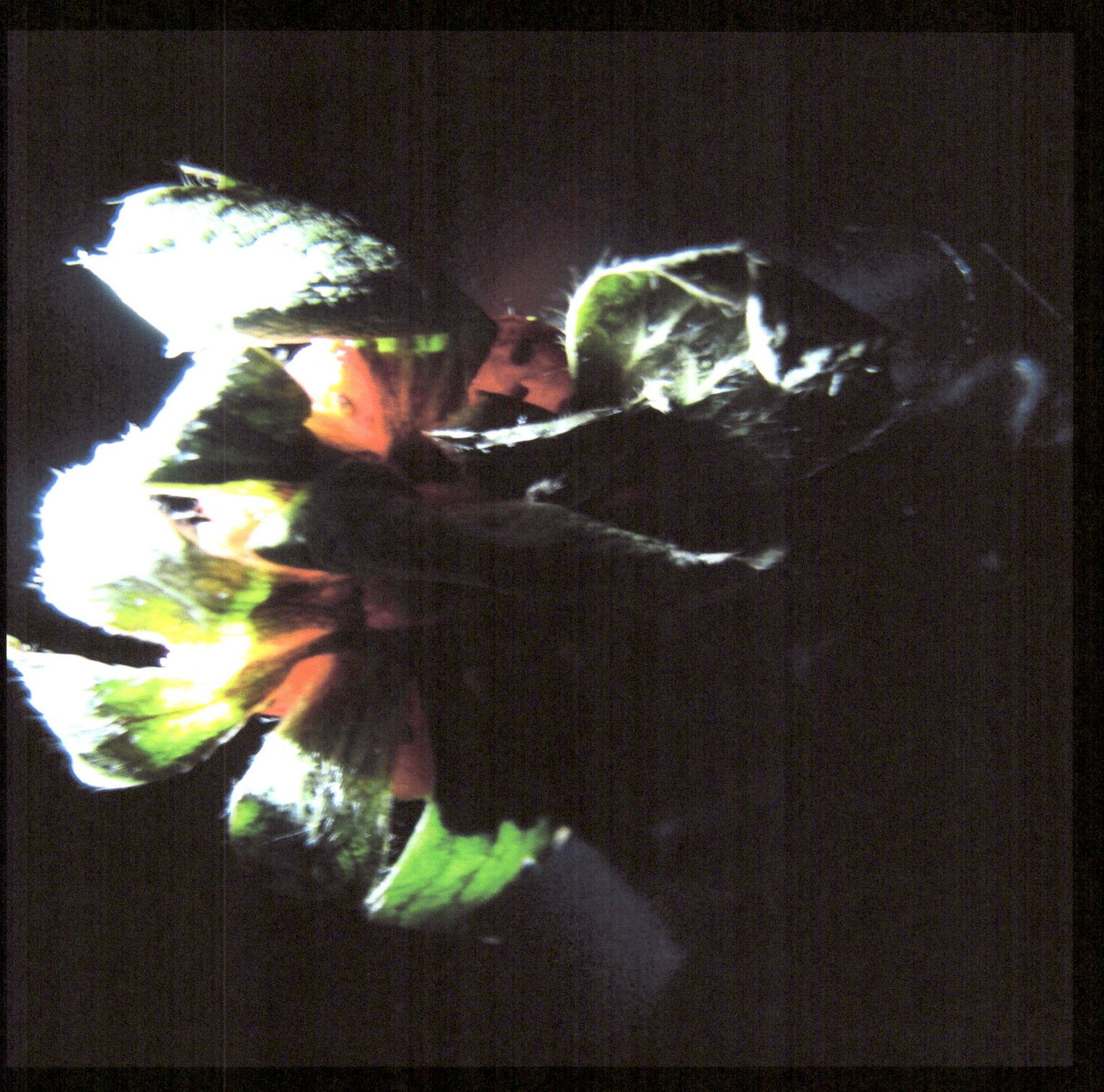

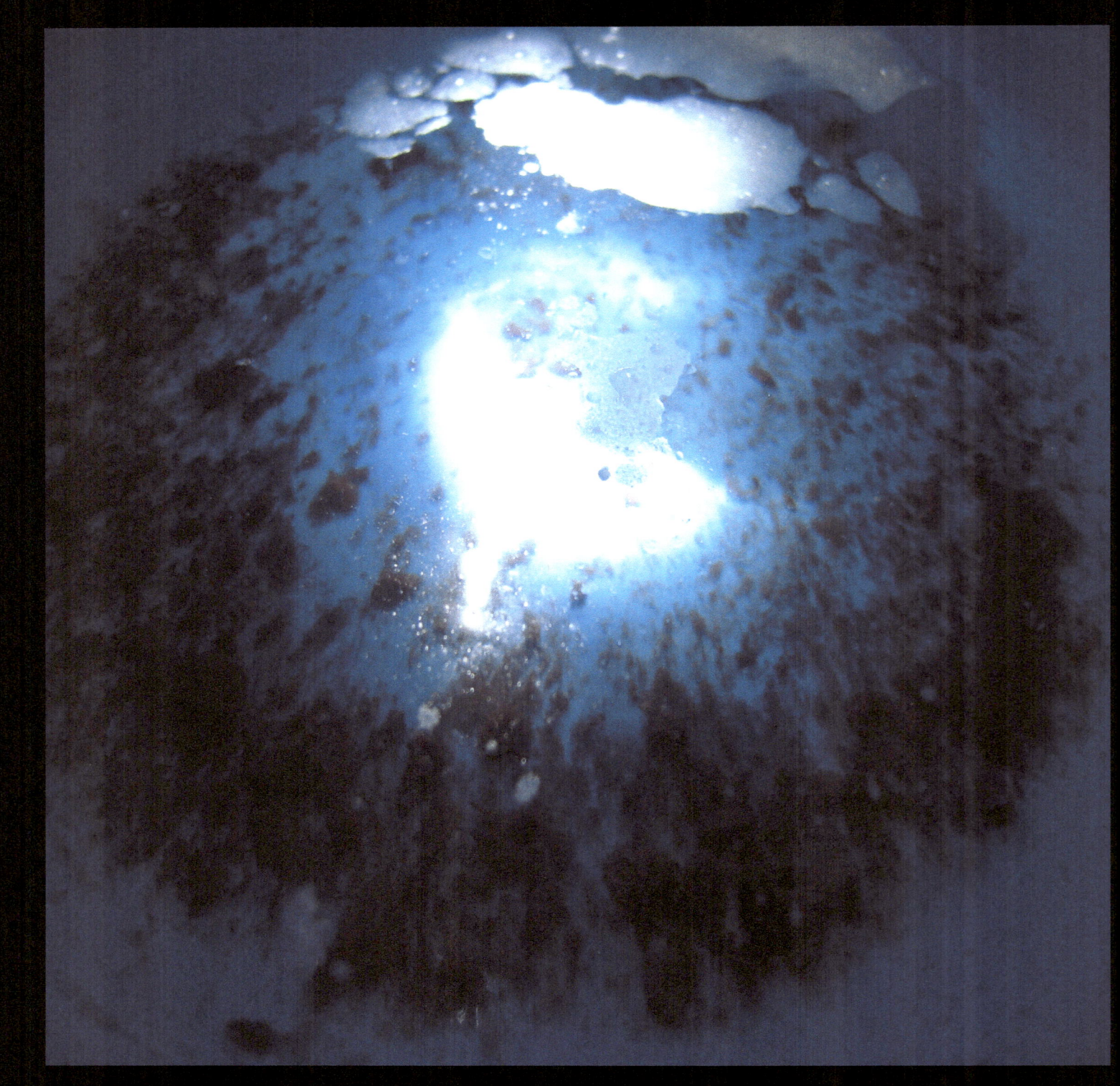

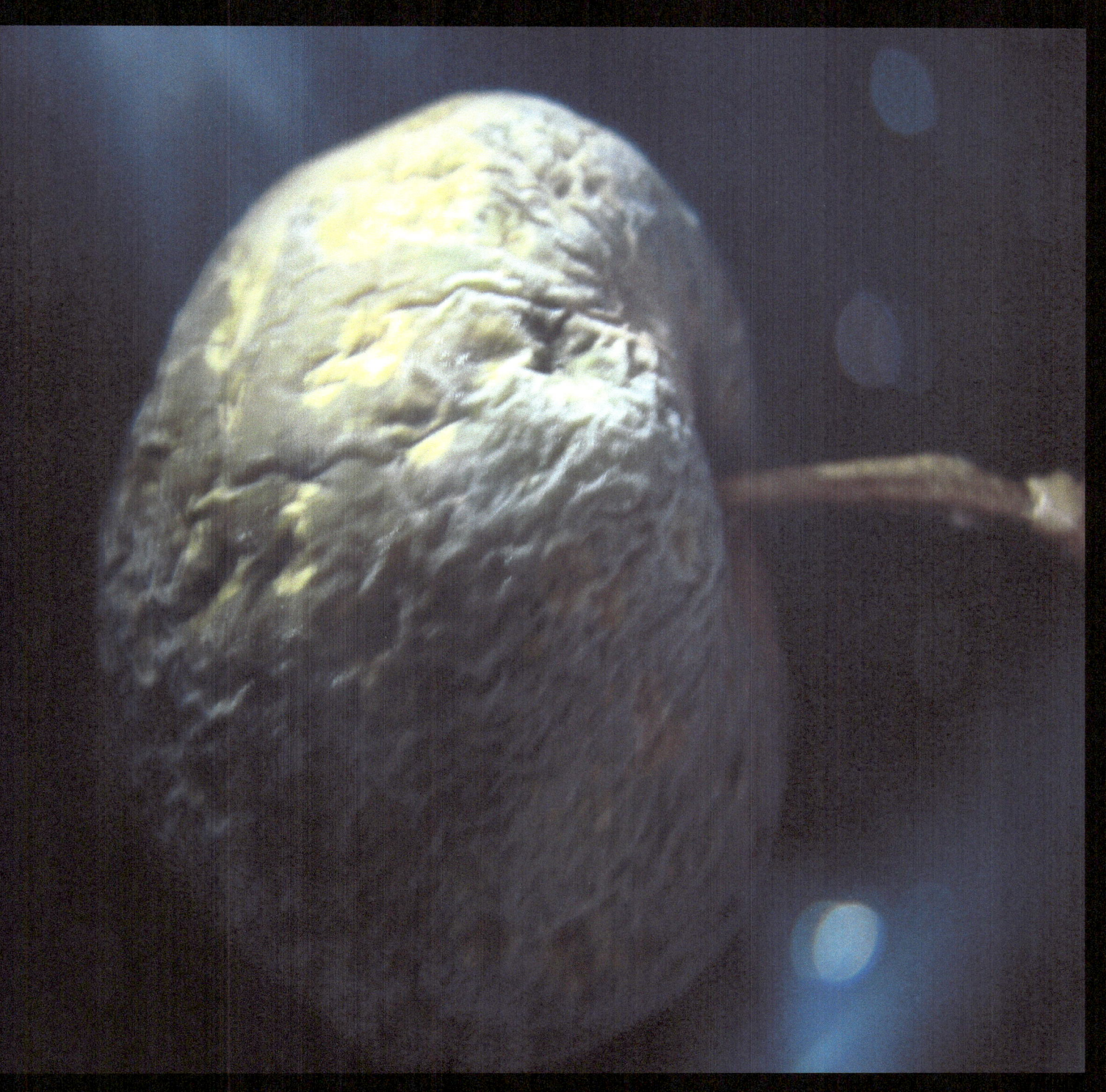

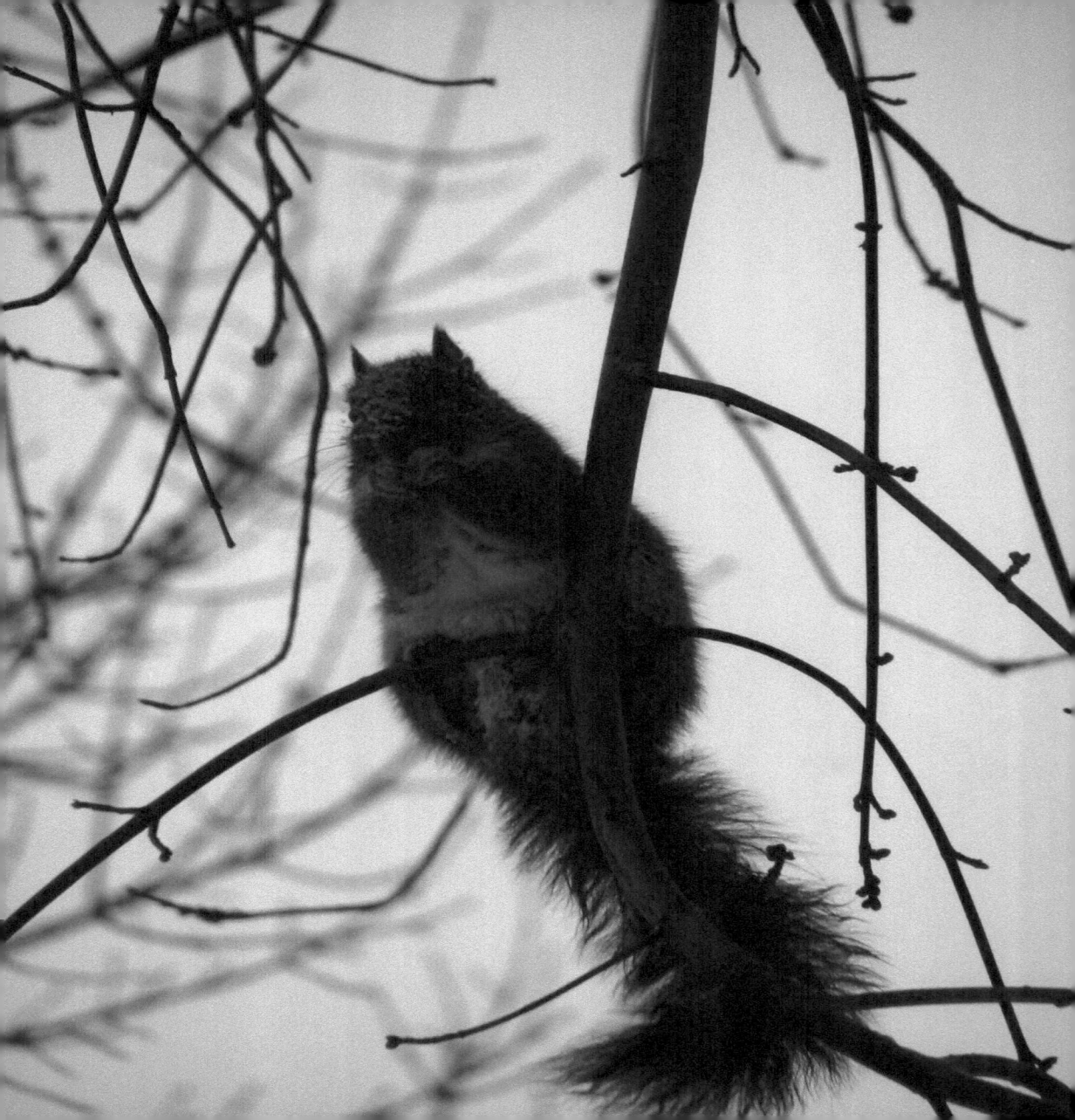

THANK YOU TO HESAKETVMESE/GOD, MY ANCESTORS

AND LOVED ONES

WHO SHOW ME HOW TO SEE MORE CLEARLY,

EVERYDAY.

THANK YOU TO MY LITTLE FRIEND

(THE SQUIRREL)

AND THE ENERGIES OF ALL

THE ITEMS USED IN THIS BOOK. YOU ARE IN MY HEART AND SOUL.

RESOURCES :

GOOD HEALTH

CREATESPACE

CANON POWERSHOT S3IS 6.0 MEGAPIXELS CAMERA

MICROSOFT PUBLISHER 2010

MINI LIGHT

ALL THINGS ARE AS THEY WHERE FOUND

OR, KEPT WITH LOVE FOR LATER.

MVTO/THANK YOU AND LOVE ONE ANOTHER

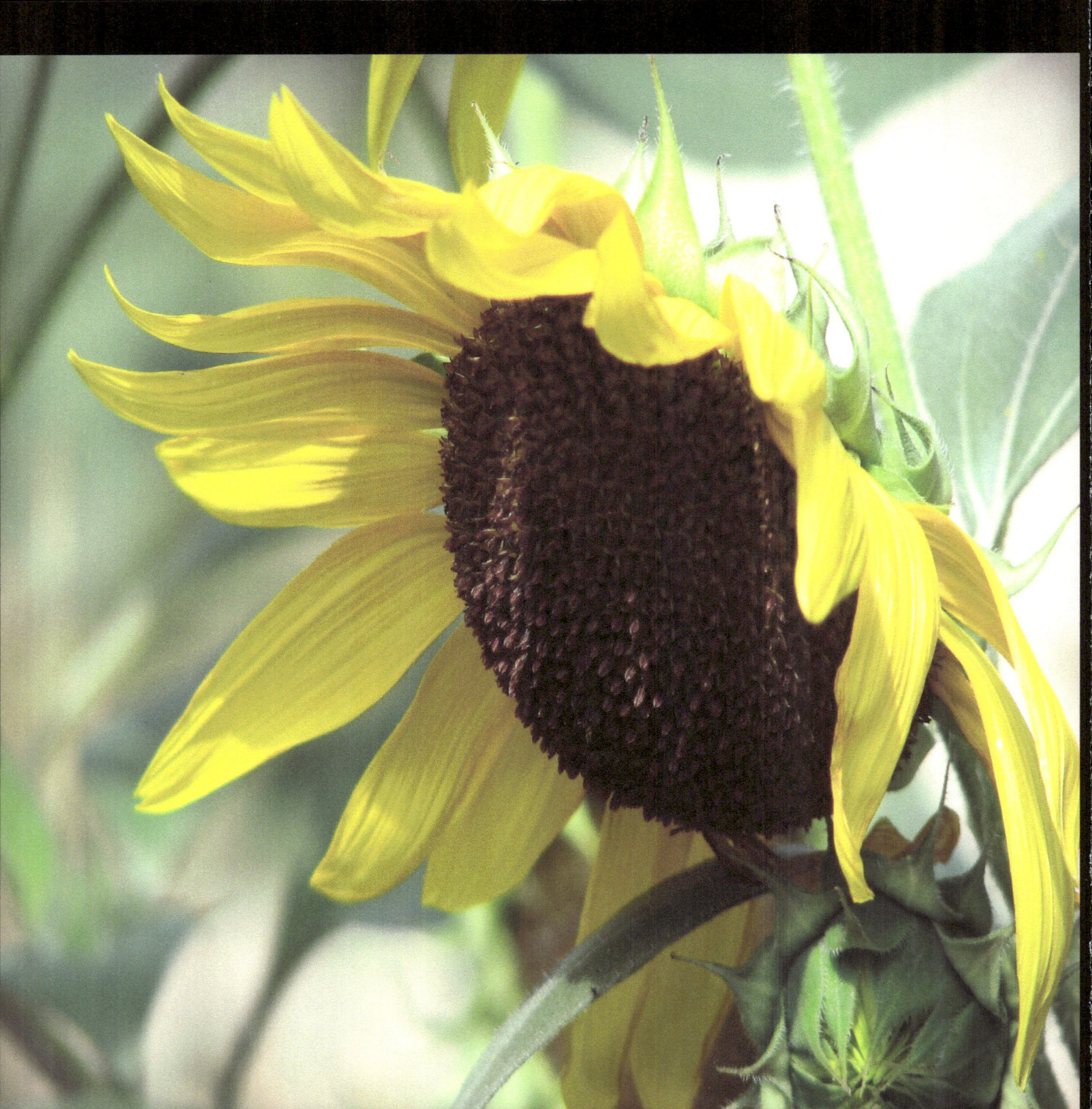